Navigating Non-Traditional Warfare:
Global Migration, Sovereignty, and Cultural Integrity

KEVIN FLINT

DEDICATION

Illegal Immigration. This should be a rather simple topic, as much of the definition is contained in the words themselves. Many would be Citizens await their chance to come to America and live the "Dream". Yet, many have taken it upon themselves to steal that dream instead and in so doing, tarnish the very concept.

Committing fraud, tax evasions and numerous other crimes, is the true face of illegal immigration. These individual that break American laws in order to cross our border steal from the average American Citizen every single day.

They engage in working whilst not paying taxes, their children attend public schools and many receive State or Federal aid, all while not paying into those systems to begin with. This places the burden and the economic expense of these individuals squarely on the shoulders of the American tax payer.

The following Act is meant as a simple framework to address these types of issues. No wall will fix them, as there are any number of ways over, or under a wall and the massive expense is also added to the illegal immigration bill that the average American has to pay.

Below I outline a system that will remove foreign-born individuals, who are in America illegally and who are currently incarcerated in State and Federal penal system and place them into a Work to Release Program.

1 National Immigration Reform Act This Program will train these individuals and place them to work for a 2 year period, working on the declining American infrastructure.

Then be returned to their own country, where they can spend 2 years working on their Countries infrastructure. The funds spent on these individuals in the Penal system and in the court system should be more than enough to cover the cost of this new program, as the funds not only already exist, but are already slated for this purpose. All this

Act does is suggest an appropriation of these existing funds to a more efficient system. The Act also covers those individuals that are not incarcerated and lays the framework for American citizenship while ensuring that their debt to the American Government and the American People, is paid in full.

Many individuals and groups, argue that the crimes committed involving illegal immigration, are small things. Yet in most States in the USA, a crime that causes more than 1,000 in damages or theft in the same amount is a Felony. It is safe to say that, in the life of the average illegal immigrant, they have committed numerous Felonies and continue to do so every year they remain with our borders.

I am not suggesting that the majority of these individuals are out being violent, or committing robberies, but Identity theft, fraud and tax evasion alone would constitute felonies in and of themselves. The hard truth is, coming across the border in a fashion not allowed by law... is a crime, the lifestyle that is demanded of illegal immigrants is fret with actions that are felonies.

2 A Proposal for Congressional Review American Citizens that break laws are expected to serve time, pay restitution, or both. I see no reason that anyone should be given a free pass. Nor would the average American give a free pass to someone who perpetrated a felony against them.

Given all of this, it hardly seems appropriate that a certain group should be excused from the law based on their country of origin, as that seems like a rather racist approach to me. America is a land of opportunity and with that opportunity comes a responsibility. Social responsibility includes paying into the American economic system, it also includes following the laws of this Country.

Allowing vast numbers of people to just walk away from numerous felonies sets a bad example, one that would serve only to encourage others to act in the same manner.

3, allowing illegal immigration to continue and encouraging it by giving free passes, also cheapens that dream for all the other people who follow the system to become an American Citizen. Should you agree with these thoughts and agree with the Act below, please write to your Senator and inform them of this work. As one voice may not be heard, but a loud enough chorus may affect some much needed change.

Thank you for your time. K. Flint

ABSTRACT

Migration, traditionally viewed through the lens of humanitarian, economic, or social phenomena, increasingly intersects with national security and sovereignty concerns, presenting both challenges and opportunities for global cooperation. The concept of migration as non-traditional warfare—a tool that can potentially be used to undermine the sovereignty and cultural integrity of nations—merits careful examination. This perspective highlights the strategic manipulation of migration flows to exert political, economic, or cultural pressure on target countries, which could lead to significant impacts on national stability and identity.

The introduction of migration as a form of non-traditional warfare necessitates a nuanced approach to understanding the multifaceted impacts of migration on national sovereignty and cultural heritage. It underscores the potential for migration to be weaponized, intentionally or unintentionally, in the geopolitical arena, thus affecting the stability and homogeneity of nation-states. This phenomenon, often referred to as "weaponized migration," poses unique challenges to the traditional paradigms of national defense and security.

Mitigating the risks associated with this form of non-traditional warfare requires a multifaceted strategy that includes global cooperation and increased awareness among nations. It calls for the establishment of robust international frameworks that can effectively manage migration flows in a way that respects the sovereignty and cultural integrity of nations while also upholding the dignity and rights of migrants. This approach necessitates a delicate balance between security concerns and humanitarian obligations, highlighting the need for innovative policy solutions that can address the root causes of forced migration, such as conflict, persecution, and economic disparities.

Global cooperation is paramount in addressing the challenges posed by weaponized migration. A collaborative international effort can facilitate the sharing of intelligence, best practices, and resources to better predict, monitor, and manage migration flows. Furthermore, raising awareness about the potential for migration to be used as a tool in non-traditional warfare can help to foster a more informed and nuanced public discourse on the subject. This, in turn, can lead to more comprehensive and compassionate policy responses that recognize the complex interplay between migration, national sovereignty, and global security.

In summary, the introduction of migration as non-traditional warfare necessitates a reevaluation of traditional concepts of national security and sovereignty. By acknowledging the potential for migration to be weaponized and adopting a proactive, cooperative approach to migration management, the international community can mitigate the risks associated with this phenomenon. This approach not only safeguards the sovereignty and cultural heritage of nations but also ensures the protection and dignity of migrants, thereby contributing to global stability and security.

Navigating Non-Traditional Warfare: Global Migration, Sovereignty, and Cultural Integrity
Chapter 1:

Navigating Non-Traditional Warfare: Global Migration, Sovereignty, and Cultural Integrity

CHAPTER: 1

Section 1.1: Defining Non-Traditional Warfare

Non-traditional warfare represents a paradigm shift in conflict strategies, moving beyond the scope of conventional military confrontations to include tactics that can destabilize nations indirectly. Among these, migration emerges as a potent tool, capable of exerting economic, social, and political pressures on receiving countries. This form of warfare leverages the movement of people across borders, not as a random or solely humanitarian phenomenon but as a strategy that can be manipulated to achieve geopolitical objectives. The strategic use of migration can strain public resources, exacerbate social tensions, and challenge the cultural and political landscapes of host nations, making it a critical aspect of modern geopolitical strategy.

Section 1.2: Challenges to Sovereignty and Cultural Heritage

The unprecedented scale of recent global migration flows poses acute challenges to the sovereignty and cultural heritage of receiving nations, particularly in the Western world. These nations are confronted with the dual imperative of upholding their humanitarian obligations to migrants and refugees, while simultaneously safeguarding their societal values, legal norms, and cultural integrity. The influx of large numbers of migrants can strain social services, impact labor markets, and stir social unrest, thereby testing the resilience of national identities and the coherence of public policies. This section will explore how nations navigate these challenges, seeking a balance between openness and the preservation of their cultural and legal frameworks in the face of changing demographics.

Section 1.3: The Catalytic Role of Non-State Actors in Migration Dynamics

1.3.1 The Diverse Spectrum of Non-State Actors:

This subsection will catalog the wide array of NSAs involved in migration, including NGOs, TNCs, migrant diaspora networks, smugglers, and international advocacy groups. Each of these actors wields influence over migration in unique ways—ranging from providing critical support services to migrants, to lobbying for policy changes at national and international levels, to facilitating illegal migration and trafficking. The section will detail how these varied activities contribute to the complex ecosystem of global migration.

1.3.2 Opportunities Presented by Non-State Actors:

Here, the discussion will focus on the positive contributions of NSAs to migration dynamics. NGOs and diaspora communities often play indispensable roles in supporting migrants through services that governments are unable or unwilling to provide. TNCs, through their labor demands and investments, can help shape migration flows in ways that potentially benefit both origin and destination countries. This subsection will argue that these actors not only provide critical support but also contribute to the economic and social integration of migrants, enriching host societies.

1.3.3 Challenges Posed by Non-State Actors:

While NSAs can offer substantial benefits, they also pose significant challenges. This subsection will address how the activities of smugglers and illicit networks threaten national security and the safety of migrants, while the advocacy efforts of some organizations may press for policy changes that conflict with national interests or societal values. The challenge lies in managing these actors in a way that protects the sovereignty and security of states while respecting the rights and needs of migrants.

1.3.4 The Need for Strategic Engagement:

Acknowledging the dual role of NSAs in migration dynamics underscores the necessity of strategic engagement. This part will argue for nuanced policy responses that recognize the beneficial aspects of NSA activities while addressing their potential to undermine national security and policy autonomy. By understanding the diverse motivations and impacts of NSAs, policymakers can develop cooperative strategies that capitalize on the opportunities presented by global migration while safeguarding against its risks.

1.3.5 Conclusion:

The introductory section concludes by underscoring the importance of a comprehensive analysis of the roles of NSAs in shaping global migration, setting the stage for the discussions that follow. It emphasizes that effective migration management and policy formulation must account for the complex interplay between state and non-state actors, striving for solutions that uphold sovereignty and security while fostering international cooperation and protecting the rights of migrants.

This expanded overview sets a detailed foundation for the subsequent exploration of global migration challenges, emphasizing the intricate roles of non-state actors in this dynamic landscape.

Chapter 2:

Historical Context of Migration Patterns

This chapter delves into the evolution of global migration patterns, tracing the roots of current trends back to historical movements of people. It examines how these patterns have shaped societies, economies, and political structures across the ages, providing a foundation for understanding the complexities of today's migration dynamics.

Section 2.1: Evolution of Global Migration

The history of human civilization is intrinsically linked to migration. From the nomadic movements of ancient peoples to the mass migrations induced by war, famine, and persecution, the flow of populations has continually reshaped the world's geopolitical and cultural landscapes.

The Roman Empire serves as an early example of how migration and the movement of peoples were central to the expansion and eventual decline of a civilization. The incorporation of diverse groups into the Roman society brought about significant economic, cultural, and technological advances but also posed challenges in terms of integration and social cohesion.

The Post-World War II period marked another significant phase in migration history, characterized by the displacement of millions of people across Europe and Asia. This period witnessed the creation of new international bodies, like the United Nations High Commissioner for Refugees (UNHCR), aimed at addressing the challenges of displacement, statelessness, and the need for asylum.

These historical precedents highlight the dual nature of migration: while it can be a driver of growth and innovation, it also poses challenges to social cohesion and governance.

Section 2.2: Recent Waves of Migration and Their Impact

In recent decades, the world has seen unprecedented levels of migration, driven by a complex interplay of factors including wars, economic disparity, and climate change.

The Syrian Civil War, beginning in 2011, has led to one of the largest refugee crises in history, with millions of Syrians displaced within their country or seeking refuge abroad. The influx of refugees into Europe and neighboring countries has tested the capacities of these nations to respond to humanitarian crises while managing integration and societal impacts.

Instability in sub-Saharan Africa, driven by conflict, economic distress, and environmental degradation, has similarly triggered significant migration flows. These movements not only impact the immediate neighboring countries but also contribute to the global migration dynamics, as people seek safer and more prosperous lives in distant lands.

The recent waves of migration underscore the urgency of developing comprehensive and humane migration policies. These policies must navigate the fine line between providing humanitarian aid to those in need and addressing the legitimate concerns of host countries regarding national interests, security, and social cohesion.

Conclusion

By examining the historical context of migration patterns, this chapter sets the stage for understanding the current challenges and opportunities presented by global migration. It underscores the importance of learning from past experiences to inform present and future responses to migration, highlighting the need for policies that are both compassionate and pragmatic, capable of addressing the complexities of a globally interconnected world.

Chapter 3:

Analyzing the Strategic Implications of Migration

This chapter explores the multifaceted strategic implications of migration, focusing on how movements of people across borders can affect geopolitical dynamics, national security, and the sovereignty of states. It considers both unintentional and deliberate uses of migration as a tool in broader strategic contexts.

Section 3.1: Migration as a Strategic Concern

Migration has emerged as a pivotal factor in international relations and strategic calculations, influencing geopolitical dynamics in profound ways. While often seen through the lens of humanitarianism or economics, migration also possesses significant strategic dimensions.

- **Geopolitical Dynamics:** Large-scale migrations can alter the demographic makeup of regions, potentially shifting political power balances. For instance, the influx of refugees into neighboring countries can strain relations, impact economic resources, and even alter the regional security landscape.

- **National Security Concerns:** The movement of people across borders presents challenges for national security, especially when it involves the unregulated flow of individuals. Issues such as the potential for the infiltration of extremists, smuggling of goods, and human trafficking are of paramount concern for states.

- **Use as a Strategic Tool:** In some instances, states have used migration deliberately as a geopolitical tool. This can involve promoting the emigration of populations to exert economic or political pressure on other countries or refusing to accept repatriation of nationals as a form of leverage.

Section 3.2: Sovereignty Under Pressure

The sovereignty of nations, a principle central to the international order, faces significant pressure in the context of global migration. The ability of a state to control its borders and manage who enters and resides within its territory is a core aspect of sovereignty.

- **Border Integrity:** Unprecedented migration flows can challenge the integrity of sovereign borders, forcing nations to reassess their border management and security strategies. This situation often requires balancing the need for security with humanitarian obligations and international legal commitments.

- **Policy Autonomy:** The pressures of migration can also impact a state's policy autonomy. International norms and agreements, such as the Refugee Convention, impose obligations on states that can limit their discretion in handling migration. Moreover, international criticism and domestic political pressures can further complicate policy decisions.

- **Impact on Internal Dynamics:** Large-scale migrations can influence the internal dynamics of receiving countries, affecting social cohesion, public services, and labor markets. These changes can provoke societal tensions, testing the resilience of national policies and the social contract between governments and their citizens.

Conclusion

The strategic implications of migration are broad and complex, intersecting with issues of national security, sovereignty, and international relations. As the global landscape continues to evolve, understanding the strategic dimensions of migration becomes crucial for policymakers. This chapter highlights the need for comprehensive strategies that address the security, humanitarian, and social implications of migration, ensuring that policies are informed by a nuanced understanding of its strategic impacts.

Chapter 4:

Sovereign Rights and Responsibilities in Managing Migration

This chapter delves into the intricate balance that nations must maintain between upholding their humanitarian obligations under international law and exercising their sovereign rights to control their borders and protect their national identity. It underscores the responsibilities that come with sovereignty, particularly in managing migration in a manner that respects human rights while ensuring national security and social cohesion.

Section 4.1: Balancing Humanitarianism with Sovereignty

The dual imperative of adhering to humanitarian principles while safeguarding sovereignty represents a significant challenge for nations in the context of global migration. This section explores the complexities involved in this balancing act, highlighting the tension between international humanitarian obligations and the sovereign right to regulate borders.

- **Humanitarian Obligations:** Nations are bound by international conventions to protect refugees and asylum seekers, ensuring their rights are respected and their needs met. This obligation often requires offering protection, assistance, and a pathway to integration for those fleeing persecution or conflict.

- **Sovereignty and Border Control:** Concurrently, states have the sovereign right to regulate the entry and residence of non-citizens, which includes establishing immigration policies, enforcing border controls, and determining the criteria for granting asylum. This right is fundamental to maintaining national security, cultural integrity, and social stability.

- **Strategic and Ethical Considerations:** The challenge lies in strategically managing migration in a way that respects human rights without compromising the state's ability to govern its territory effectively. This requires thoughtful policy frameworks that are responsive to both international obligations and domestic priorities.

Section 4.2: International Law and Sovereign Borders

This section examines the role of international law in shaping the rights and responsibilities of states regarding migration. It focuses on how the Geneva Convention and other legal instruments establish norms for the treatment of refugees and asylum seekers while recognizing the sovereignty of states.

- **Framework for Asylum and Refugee Rights:** The Geneva Convention and its protocols set forth the rights of refugees and the obligations of states to protect them. This framework is pivotal in defining legal standards for the treatment of individuals fleeing persecution.

- **National Discretion in Enforcement:** While international agreements establish broad principles, they also allow for a degree of national discretion in their implementation. This flexibility is crucial for states to balance their international commitments with their unique national contexts and security concerns.

- **Balancing Global Norms and Sovereign Laws:** The interplay between international law and national sovereignty highlights the ongoing negotiation between global norms and the domestic laws of sovereign states. It emphasizes the importance of dialogue, cooperation, and respect for diversity in approaches to managing migration.

Conclusion

Managing migration effectively requires a nuanced understanding of the interplay between sovereign rights and international humanitarian responsibilities. This chapter emphasizes the need for policies that both respect the dignity and rights of migrants and reflect the sovereign prerogatives of states. Achieving this balance is essential for fostering international cooperation, ensuring the integrity of national borders, and upholding the principles of humanitarianism in a complex and interconnected world.

Chapter 5:

Strategic Responses to Migration Pressures

In response to the multifaceted challenges posed by global migration, this chapter outlines strategic approaches that countries can adopt to manage migration pressures effectively. These strategies emphasize the importance of strengthening border security and management while also addressing the root causes of migration to create sustainable solutions.

Section 5.1: Strengthening Border Security and Management

Effective border security and management are crucial for maintaining national security and sovereignty, while also ensuring that migration is safe, orderly, and regular. This section explores innovative approaches that balance security concerns with the need to uphold humanitarian principles.

- **Technological Innovations:** The adoption of advanced technologies, including biometric verification systems, drones for surveillance, and electronic visa and asylum application processes, can enhance the efficiency and integrity of border security measures. These technologies help in accurately identifying and vetting individuals, thereby preventing unauthorized entry while streamlining the process for legitimate migrants and asylum seekers.

- **Policy Measures:** Establishing asylum processing centers outside national borders, in collaboration with international partners, can help manage asylum claims more effectively and humanely. Such centers can provide safe spaces for migrants to apply for asylum, reducing the incentive for dangerous journeys and irregular migration. Additionally, bilateral and multilateral agreements on shared border management can foster cooperation among nations, enhancing security and coordination in tackling cross-border migration challenges.

Section 5.2: Addressing Root Causes of Migration

To reduce migration pressures sustainably, it is essential to address the underlying factors that drive people to leave their homes. This section highlights the role of international cooperation in tackling these root causes.

- **Conflict Resolution:** Diplomatic efforts and peacekeeping missions aimed at resolving conflicts and building stable, peaceful societies are critical. By addressing political instability and violence, the international community can help reduce the number of people forced to flee their homes.

- **Economic Development:** Supporting economic development in countries of origin through investments, trade agreements, and development aid can create job opportunities and improve living conditions, addressing economic factors driving migration. Initiatives should focus on sustainable development, education, and skills training to foster resilient economies.

- **Climate Change Adaptation:** As climate change increasingly impacts migration, international efforts to mitigate its effects and support adaptation in vulnerable communities are crucial. This includes investing in climate-resilient infrastructure, promoting sustainable agricultural practices, and facilitating climate-induced displacement adjustments.

Conclusion

Strategic responses to migration pressures require a comprehensive approach that combines robust border management and security with proactive efforts to address the root causes of migration. By leveraging technological innovations, implementing thoughtful policy measures, and fostering international cooperation, countries can manage migration flows more effectively and humanely. This approach not only enhances national security but also contributes to global stability and prosperity, reflecting a commitment to humanitarian principles and international solidarity.

Chapter 6:

Integrating Migration into National Strategy

This chapter delves into the essential components of weaving migration policy seamlessly into the fabric of national strategy. Recognizing migration not merely as a challenge but as an opportunity, it underscores the necessity for a holistic approach that aligns migration management with broader national security and cultural objectives. This strategic integration aims to enhance social cohesion, public safety, and maintain the sovereign identity of nations while ensuring the dignified integration of migrants into society.

Section 6.1: Migration Policy as Part of National Security

The intersection of migration with national security is undeniable, with far-reaching implications for social cohesion, economic stability, and public safety. This section argues for the incorporation of proactive migration management into the national security strategy, emphasizing a multifaceted approach:

- **Risk Assessment and Preparedness:** Developing comprehensive risk assessments to understand potential security threats linked to migration, including unauthorized crossings and transnational crime, and crafting preparedness strategies to mitigate these risks effectively.

- **Interagency Coordination:** Enhancing coordination among various national agencies responsible for security, migration, and humanitarian response to ensure a unified and efficient approach to migration management.

- **International Collaboration:** Engaging in international partnerships to share intelligence, best practices, and resources, strengthening collective security and migration management efforts.

Section 6.2: Cultural Integration and Sovereignty

Balancing the cultural integration of migrants with the preservation of the host nation's cultural heritage is a delicate endeavor. This section outlines strategies to foster an environment of mutual respect and understanding, ensuring that cultural integration enriches societal fabric without eroding the cultural sovereignty of the host nation.

- **Inclusive Policies:** Developing inclusive policies that encourage the participation of migrants in social, economic, and cultural life, fostering mutual understanding and respect. Such policies should also support language learning and civic education to aid migrants in navigating their new environment.

- **Community Engagement:** Encouraging initiatives that promote interaction between migrants and host communities, such as cultural exchange programs, community dialogues, and participatory events, to build bridges and dispel myths.

- **Cultural Heritage Preservation:** Implementing programs that educate both migrants and the native population about the host country's cultural norms and values, while also celebrating and integrating the rich cultural contributions of migrants. This approach aims to build a shared sense of identity and belonging, respecting the cultural diversity of the nation.

Conclusion

Integrating migration policy into national strategy is imperative for countries navigating the complexities of contemporary migration flows. By aligning migration management with national security concerns and fostering cultural integration that respects and preserves sovereign cultural heritage, nations can harness the benefits of migration for social and economic enrichment. This strategic approach promotes a harmonious, secure, and cohesive society, ensuring that migration contributes positively to national development and global solidarity.

Chapter 7:

International Cooperation and Burden Sharing

In an era where migration has transcended the capacity of any single nation to manage effectively alone, international cooperation and burden sharing have emerged as indispensable strategies. This chapter explores the multifaceted dynamics of global collaboration in addressing migration, underscoring the pivotal role of shared responsibilities and equitable distribution of pressures to achieve sustainable solutions.

Section 7.1: Principles of International Cooperation

This section delves into the core principles that should underpin international efforts in migration management. Central to this discussion is the notion of shared responsibility, recognizing that migration is a global phenomenon requiring a collective response. Key principles include:

- **Solidarity:** Emphasizing the ethical obligation of states to support each other in managing migration flows, particularly in times of crisis.
- **Equity:** Advocating for fair and equitable sharing of responsibilities, taking into account the varying capacities and resources of different countries.
- **Respect for Sovereignty:** Ensuring that international cooperation does not impinge on the sovereign rights of states to manage their own borders, while encouraging them to adhere to international norms and standards.
- **Protection of Migrant Rights:** Prioritizing the protection of migrants' rights in all cooperative efforts, aligning with

international human rights standards.

Section 7.2: Case Studies of Burden Sharing

Through examining real-world examples, this section illustrates the practical application and benefits of burden sharing among nations. Case studies may include:

- **The EU's Relocation and Resettlement Program:** A critical analysis of the European Union's efforts to distribute the responsibility for asylum seekers among member states, examining both successes and shortcomings.
- **Regional Responses to the Syrian Refugee Crisis:** Highlighting the collaborative initiatives undertaken by countries in the Middle East and Europe to accommodate and support Syrian refugees, including financial assistance, resettlement programs, and regional agreements.

Section 7.3: Challenges and Barriers to Effective Cooperation

Despite the acknowledged benefits, numerous challenges impede effective international cooperation and burden sharing. This section identifies and discusses these obstacles, such as:

- **Lack of Political Will:** The reluctance of some nations to engage in burden sharing, often driven by domestic political considerations and nationalist sentiments.
- **Divergent National Interests:** How differing priorities and interests among countries can complicate negotiations and agreements on cooperative migration management.
- **Logistical and Financial Constraints:** The practical difficulties of implementing burden-sharing agreements, including resource allocation, logistical coordination, and the sustainable funding of collaborative projects.
- **Legal and Policy Inconsistencies:** The challenge posed by

varying legal frameworks and policies on migration across countries, complicating the harmonization of efforts.

Conclusion

The imperative for international cooperation and burden sharing in migration management is clear, driven by the complex and global nature of migration challenges. By adhering to the principles of solidarity, equity, respect for sovereignty, and the protection of migrant rights, countries can overcome barriers to effective cooperation. Success stories provide valuable lessons on the potential for collaborative approaches to redistribute pressures equitably, offering sustainable solutions that benefit both migrants and host communities. However, overcoming the persistent challenges requires renewed commitment, innovation, and the willingness to place shared humanitarian values at the heart of migration policies.

Chapter 8:

Conclusion and Recommendations for Sovereign Defense

In an increasingly interconnected world, migration presents both challenges and opportunities for sovereign nations. This chapter synthesizes the insights gained throughout the discussion and outlines a strategic approach for nations to defend their sovereignty and cultural heritage in the face of global migration pressures. It advocates for a balanced, humane approach to migration management that prioritizes national sovereignty while acknowledging the benefits of international cooperation and the imperative of upholding human dignity.

Section 8.1: Strategic Prioritization of Sovereign Defense

This section argues for the strategic prioritization of sovereign defense in the context of global migration. Key points include:

- **Sovereignty as a Fundamental Right:** Affirming the right of states to control their borders and decide on the entry and residence of non-citizens, within the bounds of international law and human rights obligations.
- **Cultural Heritage Protection:** Recognizing the importance of preserving national identity and cultural heritage amidst the dynamics of global migration, promoting policies that support cultural integration and mutual respect.
- **Balanced Migration Management:** Advocating for migration policies that balance the need for humanitarian response with the imperatives of national security and social cohesion. This includes effective border management, fair and efficient asylum procedures, and policies that address the root causes of forced migration.

Section 8.2: Call to Action for Sovereign Nations

A comprehensive call to action underscores the need for sovereign nations to adopt strategic and humane migration policies that safeguard sovereignty while contributing to global stability. Recommendations include:

- **Strengthening International Collaboration:** Encouraging nations to engage more actively in international forums and cooperative efforts to manage migration, sharing responsibilities, and resources to address common challenges.
- **Innovative Policy Solutions:** Urging the adoption of innovative policy measures that harness the benefits of migration for economic development while mitigating its potential disruptions. This could include pathways for legal migration, integration programs that promote cultural understanding, and international partnerships for development assistance in source countries.
- **Upholding Human Rights:** Emphasizing the importance of protecting the rights and dignity of migrants, irrespective of their legal status, in all policies and practices related to migration management.
- **Public Engagement and Education:** Advocating for efforts to engage and educate the public on the complexities of migration, its potential benefits, and the importance of a humane, strategic response to migration challenges.

Conclusion

The phenomenon of global migration, with its profound implications for sovereignty, security, and cultural integrity, necessitates a nuanced, strategic approach from sovereign nations. By prioritizing the defense of sovereignty and cultural heritage, while embracing the opportunities for international collaboration and innovation, nations can navigate the challenges of migration to foster global stability and prosperity. This concluding chapter calls for a commitment to strategic, humane migration policies that respect the rights of individuals and the prerogatives of nations, aiming for a future where migration is managed in a way that benefits all.

Chapter 9:

The Role of the United Nations and the International Organization for Migration in Migration Management

The intricate dynamics of global migration necessitate a coordinated, comprehensive approach that respects national sovereignty and human rights while addressing the root causes and consequences of migration. The United Nations (UN) and the International Organization for Migration (IOM) play indispensable roles in this endeavor, offering platforms, resources, and expertise for international cooperation and effective migration management.

Section 9.1: United Nations' Comprehensive Approach to Migration

The United Nations, through its specialized agencies and comprehensive reach, provides a holistic framework for addressing migration. The UN High Commissioner for Refugees (UNHCR) focuses on the protection, support, and durable solutions for refugees and forcibly displaced populations. Moreover, the UN's Sustainable Development Goals (SDGs) emphasize global cooperation to tackle migration's root causes—such as poverty, inequality, and conflict—ensuring the protection of migrant rights and promoting sustainable development.

Section 9.2: The Specialized Role of the International Organization for Migration

As the leading inter-governmental organization in the field of migration, the IOM, with its extensive member state network and global presence, plays a pivotal role in facilitating humane and orderly migration. The IOM's activities are designed to:

- Develop practical solutions to migration challenges.
- Provide humanitarian assistance to migrants in need, including refugees and internally displaced persons.
- Promote international cooperation on migration issues, thereby contributing significantly to global migration management efforts.

Section 9.3: Synergies between the UN and IOM in Migration Management

This section examines the collaborative dynamics between the UN and IOM, showcasing their joint efforts in crafting a coherent global migration governance framework. The Global Compact for Safe, Orderly and Regular Migration, a landmark intergovernmental agreement facilitated by the UN and significantly supported by the IOM, exemplifies these synergies. It aims to cover all dimensions of international migration comprehensively, marking a crucial step toward holistic and cooperative global migration management.

Section 9.4: Challenges and Opportunities for Enhanced Global Governance

Despite the achievements of the UN and IOM, global migration management faces persistent challenges, such as the need for better coordination among countries, protecting migrants' rights amidst stricter border controls, and addressing migration's root causes. This section discusses these issues and outlines opportunities for strengthening global governance on migration. Enhancing data sharing, fostering regional dialogues, and leveraging both organizations' expertise can improve migration management practices, making them more effective, humane, and equitable.

Section 9.5: Conclusion and the Path Forward

The concluding section highlights the critical roles of the UN and IOM in managing global migration and emphasizes the need for continued international cooperation. It calls for a commitment to the principles of solidarity, responsibility sharing, and respect for human rights. As the global migration landscape evolves, it is imperative for these organizations to remain engaged and adaptable, ensuring that their strategies effectively balance state sovereignty with the dignity and rights of migrants. Strengthening the global governance of migration, with the UN and IOM at the forefront, is essential for addressing current challenges and harnessing the opportunities that migration presents for societies worldwide.

Chapter 10:

Developing a Global Framework for Migration: The Role of the Global Compact for Migration

The Global Compact for Safe, Orderly and Regular Migration (GCM) represents a landmark effort in the history of global migration governance, establishing the first-ever negotiated international framework under the United Nations to address migration in all its dimensions comprehensively. This chapter explores the genesis, objectives, and implications of the GCM, alongside the challenges and prospects it holds for the international community in managing migration more effectively.

Section 10.1: Background and Genesis of the GCM

This section outlines the journey leading to the GCM's creation, highlighting the growing complexities of global migration and the international community's concerted effort to address it. The decision by the UN General Assembly in September 2016 to develop the GCM marked a critical step towards achieving a systematic and unified approach to migration, propelled by an inclusive negotiation process that embraced the insights and concerns of a diverse array of stakeholders.

Section 10.2: Core Objectives and Principles of the GCM

The chapter then delves into the GCM's 23 objectives, designed to manage migration effectively at all levels. It covers a wide spectrum of migration-related issues, from enhancing pathways for regular migration to protecting migrant rights and addressing the challenges of smuggling and trafficking. The underlying principles of the GCM, including human rights, national sovereignty, non-discrimination, and a comprehensive view of migration, form the backbone of this global framework.

Section 10.3: Implementation and Monitoring Mechanisms

An examination of the mechanisms set forth for the GCM's implementation reveals the ambitious blueprint for follow-up, review, and coordinated support through the UN Network on Migration. The section scrutinizes the Compact's reliance on voluntary and non-binding commitments, emphasizing the pivotal role of national action plans and international cooperation in fulfilling the GCM's aims.

Section 10.4: Challenges in Achieving Global Consensus

This part addresses the political contentiousness surrounding the GCM, including the withdrawal or critical stance of certain countries over concerns related to national sovereignty and border management. These divisions underscore the broader global debates on migration policy and pose significant challenges to the GCM's universal acceptance and efficacy.

Section 10.5: The Future of Global Migration Governance

Looking ahead, the section considers the GCM's potential to enhance global migration governance through fostering international cooperation and providing a comprehensive framework for addressing the multifaceted nature of migration. It stresses the necessity of ongoing adaptability, negotiation, and collaboration among stakeholders to navigate the shifting dynamics of global migration.

Section 10.6: Conclusion

In concluding, the chapter reaffirms the GCM's critical role as a milestone towards a more coordinated, cooperative approach to migration globally. It underscores the imperative for sustained engagement and commitment from all parties involved to leverage the Compact's framework for making migration a pillar of prosperity, innovation, and sustainable development worldwide.

Chapter 11:

Implementation Challenges and Future Directions

This chapter examines the multifaceted challenges involved in implementing comprehensive migration policies and outlines potential pathways forward, leveraging technology and innovation while considering the future of international migration policy.

Section 11.1: Overcoming Political and Social Hurdles

This section delves into the political and social obstacles to enacting and executing comprehensive migration policies. It highlights the critical role of public opinion, which can both propel and hinder policy advancements, depending on prevailing societal attitudes towards migrants and immigration. Political resistance, often rooted in national security concerns, economic apprehensions, or cultural preservation, further complicates the policy landscape. The necessity of cross-border cooperation is underscored, emphasizing that effective migration management requires collaborative international efforts, given the inherently transnational nature of migration. Strategies to address these challenges, including public awareness campaigns, stakeholder engagement, and international dialogue, are explored.

Section 11.2: Leveraging Technology and Innovation in Migration Management

The potential of technology and innovation to revolutionize migration management is examined in this section. It explores how artificial intelligence, big data analytics, and other technological advancements can streamline migration flows, enhance the integration of migrants into host societies, and contribute to the protection of cultural heritage. These technologies offer possibilities for more precise migration forecasting, improved efficiency in processing asylum and refugee applications, and enhanced monitoring of borders without compromising human rights. The importance of ethical considerations and the need to ensure that technological solutions do not exacerbate vulnerabilities or inequalities among migrant populations are also discussed.

Section 11.3: Future Prospects for International Migration Policy

Looking ahead, this section contemplates the evolution of international migration policy, advocating for approaches that are more equitable, efficient, and humane. It argues for policies that not only manage the challenges of migration but also harness its potential to contribute positively to global development and cultural enrichment. The discussion includes the necessity of addressing root causes of forced migration, such as conflict, climate change, and inequality, to reduce involuntary migration pressures. The section also considers the potential for international agreements and frameworks, like the Global Compact for Migration, to foster a more cooperative and coordinated global response to migration, emphasizing the importance of shared responsibility and solidarity among nations in addressing migration challenges.

Conclusion

In sum, Chapter 11 underscores the complexities involved in implementing effective migration policies but also highlights the opportunities for innovation and international cooperation. As the global landscape of migration continues to evolve, the need for adaptable, forward-looking policies that respect the rights of migrants while safeguarding national sovereignty and promoting global stability becomes increasingly apparent. By addressing political and social hurdles, leveraging technology, and envisioning a more collaborative future for international migration policy, stakeholders can work towards a more balanced, equitable, and humane migration framework for the future.

Chapter 12:

Ethical Considerations in Migration Management

This chapter delves into the ethical quandaries inherent in the management of migration, focusing on the moral implications of border control and immigration enforcement, as well as the delicate balance between cultural preservation and the integration of migrants.

Section 12.1: The Ethics of Border Control and Immigration Enforcement

This section scrutinizes the ethical challenges that nations face in enforcing border controls and immigration laws while adhering to humanitarian principles and respecting the rights of migrants. It highlights the moral dilemmas presented by policies aimed at deterring unauthorized migration, such as detention practices and the separation of families, questioning the compatibility of such measures with international human rights standards. The discussion extends to the obligations of states under international law to protect refugees and asylum-seekers, contrasting these duties with the political and societal pressures to restrict migration. This analysis encourages a reflective examination of how nations can uphold security and legality without compromising their ethical commitments to compassion, dignity, and human rights.

Section 12.2: Cultural Preservation vs. Integration

The ethical considerations surrounding the integration of migrants and the preservation of the cultural identity of host nations are debated in this section. It addresses the tension between fostering a cohesive society and respecting the multicultural diversity brought by migrants. The ethical implications of assimilation policies, which may pressure migrants to conform to the prevailing cultural norms at the expense of their own identities, are contrasted with multicultural approaches that celebrate and incorporate diversity but may also risk fostering social fragmentation. This discussion challenges readers to consider how societies can ethically navigate the complex interplay between welcoming newcomers and maintaining a sense of cultural continuity and cohesion. It advocates for policies that promote mutual respect, intercultural dialogue, and shared values as foundations for both honoring cultural heritage and facilitating successful integration.

Conclusion

Chapter 12 confronts the ethical complexities of migration management, calling attention to the need for policies that are not only effective but also morally grounded. It underscores the importance of balancing security and legality with compassion and respect for human dignity, and of finding equitable ways to celebrate cultural diversity while promoting social unity. By wrestling with these ethical considerations, policymakers, communities, and individuals can contribute to more humane and just approaches to migration that recognize the inherent worth of all people, regardless of their origin or status.

Chapter 13:

Case Studies of Migration Management

This chapter provides an in-depth analysis of different countries' experiences with migration management, examining both successful integration models and lessons drawn from failed policies. Through these case studies, readers gain insights into effective strategies and pitfalls to avoid in the complex field of migration management.

Section 13.1: Successful Integration Models

This section presents case studies of countries that have excelled in integrating migrants into their societies through innovative and compassionate policies. Examples include:

- **Canada's Express Entry System:** Canada's approach to skilled migration, emphasizing quick processing and integration into the labor market, showcases the potential for economic growth and cultural enrichment when migrants are effectively integrated.

- **Germany's Dual Vocational Training System:** Germany's program for refugees and migrants, which combines apprenticeships with vocational schooling, demonstrates the importance of aligning integration efforts with the needs of the labor market, while also providing migrants with valuable skills and social integration opportunities.

- **Sweden's Municipal Coordination:** Sweden's decentralized approach, where municipalities play a key role in the integration process, providing housing, education, and employment services, highlights the importance of local engagement and tailored support services.

Each case study explores the specific policies implemented, the challenges overcome, and the key factors contributing to their success. The lessons learned and best practices identified offer valuable insights for other nations seeking to improve their integration strategies.

Section 13.2: Lessons from Failed Migration Policies

Conversely, this section examines instances where migration policies have not achieved their intended outcomes, often exacerbating social tensions or undermining national sovereignty. Examples include:

- **The European Union's Dublin Regulation:** The regulation's principle of requiring the first country of entry to process asylum claims has placed undue pressure on border countries, leading to overcrowded reception centers and strained resources, underscoring the need for a more equitable distribution of responsibilities.

- **Australia's Offshore Processing Centers:** Australia's policy of detaining asylum seekers in offshore processing centers has drawn widespread criticism for human rights violations and poor living conditions, highlighting the ethical and humanitarian risks of such deterrent-based approaches.

- **United States' Family Separation Policy:** The U.S. policy of separating migrant children from their parents at the border served as a stark lesson in the social and psychological costs of enforcement-centric policies, emphasizing the need for humane and family-centered approaches.

Through analyzing these case studies, the section aims to extract critical lessons about the importance of upholding human rights, the need for international cooperation, and the dangers of overly punitive or deterrent-based policies. The insights gleaned from these failures are intended to inform more compassionate, effective, and sustainable migration policies in the future.

Conclusion

Chapter 13 underscores the complexity of migration management and the profound impact of policies on individual lives and national identities. By examining both successful and failed approaches, this chapter contributes to a nuanced understanding of what works and what doesn't in the quest for balanced, humane, and effective migration policies. The case studies serve as a reminder of the importance of learning from past experiences to navigate the challenges and opportunities presented by migration in a way that respects human dignity and promotes social cohesion.

Chapter 14:

Conclusion and Call to Action

In this concluding chapter, we gather the insights and recommendations developed throughout the book to underscore the urgency and necessity of a coordinated, humane approach to migration. This final chapter aims to galvanize global action towards the development and implementation of migration policies that are not only effective and ethical but also adaptable to the evolving dynamics of global migration.

Section 14.1: Synthesizing Insights for a Unified Approach

This book has explored the multifaceted nature of migration, revealing the complex interplay between economic factors, security concerns, humanitarian obligations, and the imperatives of cultural preservation and integration. Key insights include:

- **The Importance of Sovereignty and Security:** Effective migration management must reinforce the sovereignty and security of nations while ensuring that policies do not infringe on the dignity and rights of migrants.
- **The Role of International Cooperation:** The challenges and opportunities of migration are transnational in nature, requiring robust international cooperation and burden-sharing to develop solutions that are fair, efficient, and sustainable.
- **The Need for Comprehensive Policy Frameworks:** Addressing migration effectively calls for comprehensive strategies that encompass border management, integration programs, and the addressing of root causes of forced migration, such as conflict and economic disparity.

- **The Value of Innovation and Technology:** Leveraging technology and innovation can enhance the management of migration flows, improve integration processes, and facilitate the safeguarding of migrants' rights and well-being.

A unified approach to migration acknowledges these insights, striving for policies that are grounded in respect for human rights, the rule of law, and the principle of shared responsibility.

Section 14.2: A Global Call to Action

We extend a global call to action to nations, international organizations, civil society, and all stakeholders involved in the management of migration. This call to action emphasizes the following imperatives:

- **Strengthen International Collaboration:** Enhance mechanisms for international dialogue and cooperation to share responsibilities more equitably and to respond collectively to migration crises.
- **Adopt and Implement the Global Compact for Migration:** Commit to the principles and objectives of the Global Compact for Migration as a framework for international cooperation and a guide for national policy-making.
- **Innovate and Adapt:** Embrace technological advancements and innovative policy solutions to improve the efficiency, humanity, and adaptability of migration management practices.
- **Foster Inclusive Societies:** Develop integration policies that encourage social cohesion, respect cultural diversity, and support the mutual adaptation of migrants and host communities.
- **Uphold the Dignity and Rights of All Migrants:** Ensure that migration policies and practices are guided by the respect for human rights and the dignity of every individual,

irrespective of their migration status.

This call to action is rooted in the conviction that through collective effort, foresight, and compassion, it is possible to manage migration in a way that benefits all—migrants, host communities, and nations alike. It is a call for a future where migration is not seen as a challenge to be contained but as an opportunity to be embraced for the mutual benefit of humanity.

Conclusion

As we close this book, let us remember that the story of migration is ultimately the story of humanity: a story of movement, aspiration, and the search for a better life. In the face of this enduring phenomenon, our shared challenge is to craft policies and responses that reflect our common humanity and our interconnected world. The insights and recommendations offered herein are contributions towards this endeavor, a stepping stone on the path to more equitable, humane, and effective migration management for the 21st century and beyond.

Chapter 15:

Predictive Analysis and Future Trajectories in Global Migration

In this forward-looking chapter, we delve into predictive analysis to explore potential future trajectories in global migration. By examining demographic, economic, environmental, technological, and geopolitical trends, we aim to forecast how migration patterns may evolve in the coming decades and the implications for countries of origin, transit, and destination.

Section 15.1: Forecasting Future Migration Trends

Leveraging demographic data, economic forecasts, and environmental projections, this section identifies potential hotspots for increased migration flows. Factors such as aging populations in developed countries, economic disparities, and environmental degradation in developing regions are expected to drive migration trends. The implications for origin countries include potential labor shortages and brain drain, while destination countries may face challenges related to integration, infrastructure, and social cohesion.

Section 15.2: Technological Advancements and Their Impact on Migration

This section explores the transformative potential of technological advancements on migration management. Artificial Intelligence (AI) could revolutionize the processing of asylum applications and migrant data, enhancing efficiency and fairness. Blockchain technology promises to improve the verification of migrants' identities and qualifications, facilitating smoother integration into labor markets. Digital identity systems could offer undocumented migrants a pathway to accessing essential services and legal protections, fundamentally changing the dynamics of inclusion and assistance.

Section 15.3: Climate Change and Environmental Migration

As the planet warms, climate change is set to become a dominant driver of migration. This section predicts how rising sea levels, extreme weather events, and resource scarcity could force millions to relocate, challenging existing legal frameworks for migration and refugee status. The implications for traditional notions of sovereignty and national security are profound, as countries grapple with the dual challenges of protecting their borders and providing humanitarian assistance to climate-displaced populations.

Section 15.4: The Evolving Nature of Conflict and Its Influence on Migration

The nature of global conflict is changing, with an increase in cyber warfare, proxy wars, and non-state actors. This section analyzes how these shifts could impact migration patterns. The displacement of populations due to conflict is likely to continue, with new challenges arising from the strategic use of migration as a non-traditional warfare tactic. As countries navigate these complex dynamics, the international community must adapt its frameworks for protection and assistance to address the realities of modern conflict-induced displacement.

Conclusion

As we look to the future, it is clear that migration will continue to shape and be shaped by global trends. Predictive analysis offers valuable insights into the challenges and opportunities that lie ahead, underscoring the need for adaptable, forward-thinking policies. By anticipating future trends, the international community can work together to manage migration in ways that benefit both migrants and host societies, ensuring that the global migration landscape of tomorrow is navigated with humanity, cooperation, and foresight.

Chapter 16:

Regional Perspectives on Migration Management

Section 16.1: Europe's Migration Dynamics

Subsection 16.1.1: Germany

Germany has emerged as a focal point in Europe's migration dynamics, especially in the context of the Syrian refugee crisis, which saw an unprecedented number of asylum seekers arriving in Europe. The country's policies, challenges, and successes in managing migration provide crucial insights into broader European and global migration issues.

Policy and Integration Challenges: Germany's response to the influx of refugees and migrants, particularly around 2015, was marked by an initial open-door policy. Chancellor Angela Merkel's assertion "Wir schaffen das" (We can do it) underscored Germany's humanitarian stance. However, the subsequent years brought to light significant challenges, including integration into the labor market, education systems, and social services. Despite a robust framework for integration, disparities in language proficiency, employment rates, and social inclusion have persisted among migrants.

Asylum Procedures and Political Backlash: The surge in asylum applications tested Germany's administrative capacities and sparked debates over immigration, security, and national identity. The political landscape shifted as well, with a rise in support for parties critical of Merkel's migration policy. This tension highlighted the complexities of maintaining a humanitarian approach while addressing economic, social, and security concerns.

Successful Integration and Best Practices: Germany has had notable successes in integrating migrants, particularly in the labor market. Initiatives such as vocational training programs have facilitated migrants' transition into employment, contributing to the economy and fostering social cohesion. Educational programs aimed at young migrants and refugees have also played a critical role in integration.

Cross-Border Cooperation: Germany's experience underscores the importance of EU-level cooperation and burden-sharing in managing migration. The country has advocated for a common European asylum system and fair distribution of asylum seekers among member states, though progress has been slow. Germany's bilateral agreements with countries like Turkey, aimed at managing migration flows and supporting refugees in host countries, highlight the need for international cooperation beyond EU borders.

Conclusion: Germany's approach to migration management illustrates the challenges and opportunities of large-scale migration in a modern, interconnected world. The German case study provides valuable lessons in policy formulation, integration strategies, and the necessity of international cooperation. As Europe continues to navigate the complexities of migration, Germany's experiences offer insights into creating more resilient, inclusive societies.

16.1.2: France

France's approach to migration management reflects a complex interplay of history, culture, and policy, with its role in European migration governance being both pivotal and challenging. As a country with a long history of immigration, France faces unique challenges in integrating newcomers while preserving its laïcité, or secular republicanism, amidst a diverse and sometimes divided society.

Border Controls and Asylum Procedures: France's strategic location makes it a significant transit and destination country for migrants and asylum seekers. In response to increased migration flows, France has tightened its border controls and refined its asylum procedures to balance security concerns with humanitarian obligations. The establishment of hotspots and stricter asylum application reviews aim to manage arrivals more effectively, though these measures have also sparked debates about rights and access to asylum.

Historical and Cultural Context: France's colonial past and its long-standing tradition of receiving migrants have profoundly shaped its approach to migration. The principles of liberty, equality, and fraternity deeply influence its migration policies, though translating these ideals into practice is fraught with challenges. Issues around integration, secularism, and national identity frequently surface in public discourse, reflecting the ongoing struggle to define what it means to be French in a multicultural society.

Migration Policies and European Governance: France plays a crucial role in European migration governance, advocating for shared responsibility and solidarity among EU member states. Its position on issues like the reform of the Dublin Regulation, which determines the EU country responsible for processing an asylum claim, reflects a commitment to a more equitable distribution of asylum seekers. France's bilateral engagements, notably with Italy and Spain, focus on managing Mediterranean migration routes and combating human trafficking.

Integration and Social Cohesion Initiatives: France has implemented various initiatives aimed at promoting migrant integration and social cohesion. Language acquisition, access to employment, and civic integration courses are pivotal components of France's integration policy. Programs targeting educational success for children from immigrant backgrounds seek to lay the groundwork for long-term social inclusion. Despite these efforts, France continues to grapple with challenges related to discrimination, ghettoization, and unequal opportunities, indicating areas in need of significant improvement.

Areas Needing Improvement: While France has made strides in certain aspects of migration management, issues such as the lengthy asylum process, living conditions in some refugee accommodations, and instances of social exclusion underline the need for ongoing policy refinement and implementation. Strengthening the mechanisms for social inclusion, enhancing access to the labor market for asylum seekers and refugees, and addressing systemic discrimination are critical for fostering a more cohesive and resilient society.

Conclusion: France's migration management strategy, shaped by its rich historical and cultural context, is a balancing act of upholding republican values while adapting to the realities of a globalized world. The French experience highlights the importance of thoughtful policy design, robust integration efforts, and the need for continuous dialogue within society to navigate the complexities of migration in a way that strengthens social cohesion and honors the country's foundational principles.

16.1.3: Italy

Italy's geographical position in the Mediterranean makes it one of the first points of entry to Europe for many migrants and refugees. The country faces significant challenges related to irregular migration and border security, necessitating complex responses that balance humanitarian obligations with the need to regulate and manage migration flows.

Irregular Migration and Border Security: Italy is at the forefront of the European migration crisis, grappling with the arrival of migrants via perilous sea routes. The central Mediterranean route, one of the most dangerous in the world, poses significant challenges for border security and migrant safety. Italy's efforts to patrol its borders and prevent illegal crossings are complicated by the need to conduct search and rescue operations for migrants in distress at sea.

Cooperation with EU Partners and Neighboring Countries: Italy has actively sought the cooperation of EU partners and neighboring countries to manage migration flows more effectively. The country has been at the center of discussions on the reform of the Dublin Regulation, advocating for a fairer distribution of asylum seekers across the EU. Additionally, Italy has engaged in agreements with countries of origin and transit, notably Libya, to control migration flows. These agreements have been contentious, with concerns raised about the human rights conditions in Libyan detention centers.

Search and Rescue Operations: Italy has played a critical role in search and rescue operations in the Mediterranean, saving thousands of lives. The Italian Coast Guard, Navy, and NGOs have been involved in these operations, which are essential for preventing loss of life at sea. However, the involvement of NGOs in search and rescue efforts has sometimes been a point of political contention within Italy and the broader EU.

Reception of Migrants and Strain on Resources: The reception of migrants and refugees puts a significant strain on Italy's resources and infrastructure. Reception centers often struggle with overcrowding and limited resources, impacting the well-being of migrants and the ability of the authorities to process asylum applications efficiently. Italy has called for more solidarity and support from the EU to share the burden and ensure that migrants are treated humanely and with dignity.

Conclusion: Italy's position in the Mediterranean places it at the heart of the migration challenge facing Europe. The country's efforts to manage irregular migration, ensure border security, and save lives at sea are crucial aspects of the broader European response to migration. Italy's experience underscores the need for enhanced cooperation and solidarity among EU member states and with neighboring countries to develop sustainable, humane solutions to migration challenges.

16.1.4: Spain

Spain, like Italy, is another frontline state in the EU facing significant migration pressures, primarily through its territories in North Africa (Ceuta and Melilla) and across the Mediterranean Sea. Its geographical position has made it both a transit and destination country for migrants from North Africa and sub-Saharan Africa.

Irregular Migration Flows Across the Mediterranean: Spain's migration challenges are characterized by irregular migration flows across the Mediterranean and attempts to cross overland into Ceuta and Melilla. These routes are perilous and have led to numerous tragedies at sea and at the borders of Spain's North African enclaves. Spain has implemented a range of measures to manage these flows, including rescue operations at sea to safeguard lives.

Cooperation with North African Countries: A pivotal aspect of Spain's migration strategy involves cooperation with North African countries, notably Morocco, from where many migrants attempt to reach Spain. These agreements focus on border management, combating human trafficking networks, and addressing root causes of migration in origin countries. While effective in reducing irregular entries, these partnerships have raised concerns regarding the treatment of migrants and asylum seekers in transit countries.

Spain as a Transit and Destination Country: Spain's dual role as a transit and destination country complicates its migration management strategy. While many migrants aim to reach other European countries, a significant number remain in Spain, seeking asylum or opportunities to work. Spain has worked within the EU framework to advocate for responsibility sharing among member states, pushing for reforms to the Dublin Regulation that would alleviate the burden on frontline countries.

Successful Integration Initiatives: Despite the challenges, Spain has implemented several successful integration initiatives aimed at facilitating the social and economic inclusion of migrants. These include language training, employment programs, and measures to ensure access to healthcare and education. Local communities and NGOs play a crucial role in these efforts, often supported by EU funds.

Need for Enhanced Cooperation at the EU Level: Spain's experience highlights the need for enhanced cooperation at the EU level to address migration challenges effectively. This includes not only fairer distribution of asylum seekers among member states but also increased financial and operational support for frontline countries. Moreover, a comprehensive approach to migration should address root causes in origin countries and ensure the protection of human rights throughout the migration process.

Conclusion: Spain's approach to managing migration reflects the complex dynamics of being a frontline state in the EU. Its efforts to balance border security with humanitarian responsibilities, cooperation with North African partners, and the integration of migrants underscore the multifaceted nature of migration challenges. Spain's experience reinforces the importance of solidarity and shared responsibility within the EU to develop sustainable, humane responses to migration.

16.1.5: Sweden

Sweden's migration policies have been notable for their generosity and openness, particularly in terms of asylum and refugee resettlement. This Nordic country has been among the EU states offering the most significant support to refugees per capita, showcasing a strong commitment to humanitarian principles. However, the substantial influx of asylum seekers, especially during the 2015 crisis, has tested Sweden's capacities and approaches to integration and social cohesion.

Asylum and Refugee Resettlement: Sweden's approach to asylum and refugee resettlement has historically been characterized by a high level of acceptance and support for people fleeing conflict and persecution. The country offers a comprehensive resettlement program, providing refugees with access to housing, education, and integration services. However, the dramatic increase in asylum applications in 2015 led to a tightening of asylum laws and border controls, reflecting the challenges in sustaining such a welcoming stance amidst significant numbers.

Integration and Social Cohesion: Integration has been a central concern for Sweden, given its relatively high number of asylum seekers and refugees. The country has invested in language training, employment initiatives, and education to facilitate newcomers' integration into Swedish society. Despite these efforts, Sweden has faced challenges related to social cohesion, including difficulties in employment for refugees compared to native Swedes and tensions in certain communities. However, successful practices, such as local community engagement and targeted support programs, have shown promising results in promoting inclusion.

Role in European Migration Debates: Sweden has been an active participant in European migration debates, advocating for a common EU asylum system and greater solidarity among member states in sharing the responsibility for refugees. The Swedish government has called for a fair distribution of asylum seekers across the EU, emphasizing the need for a coordinated approach to address the root causes of forced migration. Sweden's experience with both the benefits and challenges of a generous asylum policy positions it as a crucial voice in discussions on reforming the EU's migration and asylum policies.

Efforts to Promote Solidarity and Responsibility-Sharing: In the face of rising migration pressures on the EU, Sweden has underscored the importance of solidarity and shared responsibility among member states. This includes financial contributions to EU funds supporting frontline states, participation in EU relocation schemes, and diplomatic efforts to advance a more unified and humane approach to migration within the bloc. Sweden's advocacy for a holistic approach to migration management, emphasizing human rights and the need for long-term solutions, reflects its commitment to playing a constructive role in shaping EU policies.

Conclusion: Sweden's experiences with migration, from its open asylum policies to the challenges of integration and social cohesion, highlight the complexities of managing migration in a way that balances humanitarian responsibilities with social and economic realities. As Sweden continues to navigate these challenges, its role in advocating for EU-wide solutions and responsibility-sharing remains critical. The Swedish case underscores the necessity of comprehensive and collaborative approaches to migration that safeguard the rights and dignity of all individuals while ensuring the cohesion and resilience of host societies.

16.1.6: Netherlands

The Netherlands presents a unique case in European migration governance, blending stringent asylum procedures with a strong commitment to international refugee assistance and innovative integration strategies. The Dutch approach to migration is characterized by a pragmatic balance between securing borders, fulfilling humanitarian obligations, and facilitating the successful integration of newcomers into society.

Asylum, Integration, and Border Management: Dutch migration policies have traditionally been among the more progressive in the EU, with a focus on the rights of asylum seekers and refugees. The Netherlands employs rigorous but fair asylum procedures aimed at quickly identifying genuine refugees for protection while deterring unfounded claims. Integration is a cornerstone of Dutch migration policy, with newcomers required to participate in language and civic integration courses shortly after their arrival. The government also emphasizes labor market integration, recognizing the mutual benefits of facilitating migrants' transition into employment.

Role in EU's Migration Governance: The Netherlands plays a proactive role in the EU's migration governance, advocating for a balanced approach that combines responsibility-sharing with the protection of external borders. Dutch policy has been influential in shaping EU discussions on migration, particularly in areas such as border management, asylum system reform, and the development of common return policies for migrants not eligible for protection. The Netherlands often seeks to bridge gaps between EU member states with diverging views on migration management.

Cooperation with Neighboring Countries: Bilateral and regional cooperation forms a significant aspect of Dutch migration policy. The Netherlands works closely with neighboring countries and countries of origin and transit to manage migration flows, combat human trafficking, and improve conditions in refugee camps. Such cooperation is often framed within broader EU efforts to address the root causes of forced migration through development aid, conflict resolution, and capacity-building initiatives.

Innovative Integration Programs: The Netherlands has been a pioneer in developing innovative integration programs that not only focus on language and employment but also aim to foster cultural understanding and social cohesion. These include mentorship schemes pairing newcomers with local residents, community-based projects to encourage interaction between migrants and host communities, and targeted support for refugee entrepreneurs. These efforts reflect a comprehensive view of integration as a two-way process involving both migrants and the receiving society.

Contributions to International Refugee Assistance: Beyond its borders, the Netherlands contributes significantly to international refugee assistance and resettlement efforts. The Dutch government supports UNHCR and other international organizations in providing humanitarian aid to refugees and displaced persons worldwide. It also participates in international resettlement programs, offering a new home to refugees identified by UNHCR as in need of resettlement based on vulnerability criteria.

Conclusion: The Netherlands' migration policies exemplify a multifaceted approach that seeks to balance border security, humanitarian obligations, and the successful integration of migrants and refugees. Through its active role in EU migration governance and innovative domestic initiatives, the Netherlands demonstrates the potential for policies that are both pragmatic and principled, contributing to more effective and humane migration management at both the European and global levels.

16.1.7: Greece

Greece occupies a critical position in the European migration landscape, acting as one of the first points of entry for many migrants and refugees attempting to reach the EU via the Eastern Mediterranean route. The country has faced significant challenges in managing irregular migration across the Aegean Sea, compounded by the geopolitical complexities of its location and the protracted nature of conflicts in the Middle East and Africa.

Irregular Migration and Migrant Arrivals: The Aegean Sea islands have been the epicenter of Greece's migration challenges, witnessing dramatic increases in migrant arrivals during peak periods of the migration crisis. Greece's geographical proximity to Turkey makes it a preferred entry point for migrants and refugees attempting to reach Europe. The country has struggled to balance humanitarian responsibilities with the need to manage and regulate these arrivals effectively.

Cooperation with the EU and Neighboring Countries: Greece's response to migration challenges has been shaped in close cooperation with the EU and neighboring countries. The EU-Turkey Statement of March 2016 aimed to reduce irregular migration to Greece by allowing the return of migrants arriving on the Greek islands back to Turkey. While controversial, this agreement led to a significant decrease in arrivals. Furthermore, Greece has received substantial financial and operational support from the EU and agencies such as Frontex to enhance border control, asylum procedures, and migrant reception capacities.

Strain on Resources and Infrastructure: The surge in migrant arrivals has placed immense strain on Greece's resources and infrastructure, particularly on the Aegean islands, where reception facilities have often been overwhelmed. Conditions in some reception centers have been criticized by international organizations and NGOs for being below international standards, with overcrowding, inadequate shelter, and limited access to services being recurrent issues.

Improving Reception Conditions and Compliance with International Standards: In response to these challenges, Greece has undertaken efforts to improve reception conditions and ensure compliance with international and EU standards. These efforts include the construction of new reception and identification centers with better facilities, the acceleration of asylum procedures to alleviate overcrowding, and initiatives to enhance migrants' access to healthcare, education, and integration services. Additionally, Greece has worked on decongesting the islands by transferring asylum seekers to the mainland, where conditions are generally better.

Conclusion: Greece's experience highlights the complex interplay of geographic, political, and humanitarian factors in managing migration flows. Despite facing significant challenges, Greece has made strides in improving the management of migrant arrivals, in cooperation with the EU and other stakeholders. The situation underscores the importance of shared responsibility, solidarity, and cooperation among EU member states and with neighboring countries to address the multifaceted challenges of migration in a way that is humane, respects the rights of migrants and refugees, and ensures the security and well-being of host communities.

16.2.1: United Kingdom

The United Kingdom's migration policies have undergone significant transformations, especially in the wake of Brexit. The country's approach to immigration, asylum, and refugee resettlement is now navigating through a period of redefinition and adjustment to its new status outside the European Union.

Immigration, Asylum, and Refugee Resettlement: The UK has traditionally been a prime destination for migrants, asylum seekers, and refugees due to its strong economy, established legal system, and comprehensive welfare state. The country's policies have oscillated between openness to skilled migrants and a tightening of rules around asylum to deter irregular migration. In recent years, the government has introduced a points-based immigration system aimed at attracting 'high-skilled' workers while restricting lower-skilled immigration, reflecting a broader shift towards more selective admission criteria.

Impact of Brexit on Migration Dynamics: Brexit has fundamentally altered the UK's migration dynamics, especially its relationship with the EU regarding freedom of movement. The end of freedom of movement for EU citizens has marked a significant policy shift, requiring both British and European citizens to navigate new immigration rules. This change impacts various sectors, from healthcare to agriculture, that have historically relied on EU labor. Additionally, Brexit has implications for the Dublin Regulation, which previously allowed the UK to transfer asylum seekers to the first EU country they had entered, raising questions about future cooperation on asylum and border control.

Challenges and Opportunities in Addressing Migration Issues: Post-Brexit, the UK faces numerous challenges in managing migration, including the need to balance labor market demands with public concerns about immigration. The country must also address the integration and social cohesion of migrants, ensuring that newcomers have access to services and opportunities to contribute to their communities. There is an opportunity for the UK to craft an independent migration policy that meets its specific needs while upholding international obligations and human rights standards.

Integration and social cohesion remain pivotal, with initiatives aimed at supporting the inclusion of migrants into British society being critical for harmonious community relations. The government and local communities play essential roles in facilitating integration through language education, employment opportunities, and social engagement activities.

Conclusion: The United Kingdom stands at a crossroads, with Brexit offering an opportunity to redefine its approach to migration. While challenges exist, particularly around integration and adapting to new migration dynamics, there are also opportunities to develop policies that are fair, meet economic needs, and respect the rights of migrants. The effectiveness of the UK's migration policies in this new era will depend on its ability to balance domestic priorities with its international commitments and the changing global migration landscape.

16.2.2: Canada

Canada's immigration system is often lauded for its structured approach to selecting immigrants, including a points-based selection system that prioritizes skilled workers, and its commitment to humanitarian resettlement programs. The country has a long history of welcoming immigrants and refugees, which is reflected in its diverse and multicultural society.

Points-Based Selection and Humanitarian Resettlement: Canada's immigration policy is built around a points-based system that assesses potential immigrants based on factors such as language proficiency, education, work experience, and adaptability. This system aims to attract individuals who will contribute economically to the country. Alongside economic immigration, Canada has a strong commitment to resettling refugees through government-assisted and private sponsorship programs, demonstrating a balanced approach to fulfilling both economic needs and humanitarian obligations.

Immigration and Refugee Integration: Canada is recognized for its successful integration policies, which include comprehensive settlement services like language training, employment assistance, and community support. These services are designed to help newcomers adjust to life in Canada and become active, contributing members of society. Despite these efforts, challenges remain, including the recognition of foreign credentials, access to affordable housing, and ensuring equitable opportunities for all immigrants and refugees, regardless of their origin or economic class.

Contributions to International Refugee Assistance and Global Migration Governance: Canada plays a significant role in international refugee assistance, not only by resettling a significant number of refugees but also by sharing its expertise and practices in refugee integration with other countries. Canada's approach to private sponsorship of refugees, where private citizens and community groups take on the responsibility of supporting resettled refugees, is a model that has inspired other nations to adopt similar programs.

Furthermore, Canada actively participates in global migration governance, advocating for safe, orderly, and regular migration. The country is a key player in international forums discussing migration and refugee issues, promoting policies that support global cooperation and responsibility-sharing among nations.

Conclusion: Canada's approach to immigration and refugee resettlement stands as a testament to its values of diversity, inclusion, and humanitarianism. While the system is not without its challenges, particularly in ensuring equal opportunities for all newcomers, Canada's policies and practices offer valuable lessons for other countries grappling with migration management. By continuing to refine its approach and working collaboratively on the international stage, Canada can maintain its position as a leader in welcoming and integrating immigrants and refugees into its society.

16.2.3: Australia

Australia's migration policies are a complex blend of strict border control measures, including offshore processing and detention of asylum seekers, alongside a points-based system for skilled migration that seeks to meet the nation's economic needs. This dual approach reflects Australia's efforts to manage its borders while also recognizing the benefits of skilled immigration.

Offshore Processing and Detention: Australia's policy of offshore processing and detention for asylum seekers arriving by boat has been one of the most contentious aspects of its migration strategy. Implemented with the aim of deterring irregular maritime arrivals, asylum seekers are processed in facilities located outside Australia's territory. Critics argue that these policies compromise human rights and the dignity of individuals seeking protection, leading to international scrutiny and calls for reform.

Points-Based Immigration System: Parallel to its strict asylum policies, Australia operates a points-based immigration system designed to attract skilled migrants who can contribute to the country's economic growth. This system assesses candidates on factors such as age, language proficiency, work experience, and education, allowing Australia to tailor its intake of immigrants to the evolving needs of its economy.

Challenges and Controversies: Australia's migration policies have faced criticism both domestically and internationally, particularly concerning the treatment of asylum seekers and the conditions in offshore detention centers. These issues have sparked a national debate on the balance between border security and Australia's obligations under international human rights law. Additionally, while the points-based system has generally been successful in attracting skilled migrants, there have been challenges in ensuring that all immigrants, regardless of their pathway to Australia, have opportunities for successful integration and access to employment in their fields.

Regional Migration Management and Human Rights: Australia has sought to address irregular migration by engaging in regional cooperation and agreements aimed at managing migration flows and combating human trafficking and smuggling. The country has also made efforts to resettle refugees from regional processing centers to third countries, although these efforts have often been met with logistical and political challenges.

Furthermore, Australia has contributed to international discussions on migration and refugee protection, advocating for a comprehensive approach to managing migration that includes addressing root causes, enhancing regional cooperation, and ensuring that migration policies respect human rights standards.

Conclusion: Australia's migration policies represent a delicate balance between controlling its borders and fulfilling its economic and humanitarian commitments. While the points-based immigration system has been effective in attracting skilled workers, the offshore processing and detention policies have faced significant criticism. Moving forward, Australia faces the challenge of maintaining its sovereignty and security while ensuring that its policies uphold international standards of human rights and dignity for all individuals seeking refuge and opportunity within its borders.

Chapter 17:

Navigating the Challenges of Unauthorized Migration in America

Section 17.1: The Historical and Present Challenge of Unauthorized Immigration

17.1.1: Overview of the Evolution of Unauthorized Immigration into America

The history of unauthorized immigration into the United States is a complex tapestry woven through the nation's economic, political, and social fabric. Early migrations, driven by the demand for labor and the allure of freedom and opportunity, set the stage for patterns of unauthorized immigration that have evolved over centuries. This evolution has been significantly shaped by legislation and economic demands, reflecting the changing needs and attitudes of the country.

Early Migrations and Legislative Responses: Prior to the 20th century, migration to the United States was relatively unrestricted. However, as the country industrialized and urbanized, concerns over the impact of immigration on society and the labor market began to grow, leading to the first immigration restrictions. The Chinese Exclusion Act of 1882 was among the earliest examples, targeting a specific group based on nationality.

The Bracero Program and Shifts in Policy: The Bracero Program (1942-1964) marked a significant period where temporary labor needs during and after World War II led to the recruitment of Mexican agricultural workers. While this program allowed for legal migration, it also set the precedent for future patterns of labor migration and the challenges of unauthorized immigration that would follow its end.

The Immigration and Nationality Act of 1965: This landmark legislation abolished the national origins quota system and established a new immigration policy based on reunifying families and attracting skilled labor to the United States. While it opened up legal channels for immigration from countries previously restricted, it also inadvertently contributed to a rise in unauthorized immigration by imposing limits on Western Hemisphere immigration for the first time, creating backlogs and bottlenecks in the legal immigration process.

Impacts of NAFTA in the 1990s: The North American Free Trade Agreement (NAFTA) had profound effects on migration patterns, particularly from Mexico. While it aimed to create economic opportunities by eliminating trade barriers, it also disrupted local economies, particularly in agriculture, leading many to seek employment opportunities in the United States. This economic dislocation contributed to an increase in unauthorized immigration during the 1990s and early 2000s.

Statistical Trends and Policy Shifts: The number of unauthorized immigrants in the United States grew steadily from the 1980s, peaking in the mid-2000s. Since then, the numbers have stabilized and even declined, according to estimates from the Department of Homeland Security and independent research organizations. This trend reflects a combination of factors, including the Great Recession, improvements in the Mexican economy, and heightened U.S. border enforcement.

Policy responses over time have oscillated between enforcement-centric approaches and efforts towards comprehensive immigration reform. Initiatives such as the Deferred Action for Childhood Arrivals (DACA) program have sought to address specific aspects of unauthorized immigration, while broader legislative reforms have faced significant political hurdles.

Conclusion: The evolution of unauthorized immigration into America is a reflection of broader socio-economic dynamics and policy decisions. Understanding this history is crucial for developing informed and effective responses to the challenges of unauthorized immigration today. The interplay between economic demands, legislative action, and global economic forces underscores the complexity of immigration issues, necessitating a nuanced and multifaceted policy approach.

17.1.2: Analysis of Current Unauthorized Immigration Trends

The landscape of unauthorized immigration in the United States today is markedly different from that of previous decades, shaped by a complex interplay of demographic shifts, technological advancements, policy changes, and global socio-economic dynamics. Understanding the current trends requires a deep dive into the motivations, demographics, and experiences of unauthorized immigrants, as well as the external factors influencing migration patterns.

Demographics and Motivations: Recent unauthorized immigration to the United States is characterized by significant diversity in terms of national origin, age, and socioeconomic background. While Mexicans have historically constituted the largest group among unauthorized immigrants, recent years have seen an increase in migrants from Central America, Asia, and Africa. The motivations behind their migration are varied but often include fleeing violence and persecution, escaping poverty, reuniting with family, or seeking better educational and economic opportunities. The decision to migrate is rarely taken lightly and is often seen as a last resort to achieve safety and stability.

Impact of Technology: Technology plays a dual role in unauthorized immigration, acting both as a facilitator for migrants and a tool for enforcement agencies. Social media and mobile technology provide platforms for migrants to share information on routes, dangers, and legal advice, forming virtual communities that span across countries. However, technology also enables more sophisticated surveillance and tracking methods at borders, increasing the risks and challenges for those attempting to cross into the United States without authorization.

Heightened Border Security: The significant fortification of the U.S.-Mexico border, marked by the construction of barriers, deployment of advanced surveillance technology, and increased personnel, has altered migration patterns. While it has made crossing more difficult in traditional urban entry points, it has pushed migrants to more dangerous and remote areas, increasing the perils of the journey. Moreover, the militarization of the border has contributed to a rise in the use of smuggling networks, making migration more expensive and perilous.

Shifting Patterns Due to Policy Changes: Policies such as the Deferred Action for Childhood Arrivals (DACA) program have had profound effects on migration dynamics. DACA, which offers temporary relief from deportation and work authorization to eligible young unauthorized immigrants, has influenced decisions around migration, particularly among families with mixed immigration statuses. However, the uncertain future of such programs adds to the anxiety and unpredictability faced by unauthorized immigrants.

Economic Forces and Migration Flows: Economic conditions in both the United States and countries of origin continue to be a significant driver of unauthorized immigration. Improvements in the economies of origin countries can reduce the push factors for migration, while economic downturns and lack of opportunities can exacerbate them. In the United States, the demand for labor in certain sectors, such as agriculture, construction, and service industries, continues to attract unauthorized workers, despite the risks involved.

Conclusion: The current trends in unauthorized immigration are the result of a multifaceted set of factors that include not only individual motivations and aspirations but also broader political, economic, and technological changes. Understanding these trends requires a holistic approach that considers the myriad forces at play and the human stories behind the statistics. As policies and conditions evolve, so too will the patterns of unauthorized immigration, underscoring the need for adaptive and informed policy responses.

17.1.3: Examination of the Public Safety, National Security, and Health Concerns

The discourse around unauthorized immigration often intersects with issues of public safety, national security, and public health, each becoming a focal point in debates on immigration policy. An evidence-based examination of these concerns is crucial to dispelling prevalent myths and shaping informed, effective policies.

Public Safety and National Security Concerns: Common narratives sometimes unfairly associate unauthorized immigration with increased crime rates and security threats. However, a breadth of research indicates that immigrants, regardless of legal status, are less likely to commit crimes than native-born citizens. Studies have consistently shown that areas with higher concentrations of immigrants experience lower rates of crime. This counterintuitive finding suggests that unauthorized immigrants are, on the whole, contributing members of their communities who seek to avoid legal troubles that could jeopardize their ability to remain in the U.S.

When it comes to national security, unauthorized immigration is often conflated with the risk of terrorism. Yet, rigorous security screenings for refugees and the lack of empirical evidence linking unauthorized immigrants to terrorism challenge the validity of this association. The focus on unauthorized immigration as a primary national security threat may divert attention and resources from more effective measures to protect against terrorism, such as intelligence gathering and international cooperation.

Public Health Implications: Unauthorized immigrants are often excluded from health insurance and public health services, a situation that can have far-reaching implications beyond the individuals directly affected. The COVID-19 pandemic has underscored the interconnectedness of community health, demonstrating that viruses and other health threats do not respect legal statuses. Excluding a segment of the population from healthcare and public health initiatives can hinder efforts to control the spread of infectious diseases, ultimately putting the entire population at greater risk.

Moreover, the fear of deportation may deter unauthorized immigrants from seeking medical care or participating in public health efforts, such as vaccination campaigns, contact tracing, or testing programs. This not only exacerbates their vulnerability to health issues but also poses a broader public health risk.

Incorporating unauthorized immigrants into public health strategies is essential for comprehensive community health safety. Ensuring access to healthcare, preventative services, and public health initiatives for all residents, regardless of immigration status, can improve public health outcomes, reduce emergency healthcare costs, and facilitate the early detection and treatment of infectious diseases.

Conclusion: Addressing the concerns related to public safety, national security, and public health in the context of unauthorized immigration requires a nuanced understanding that goes beyond stereotypes and myths. Evidence-based policies and inclusive public health strategies are crucial for fostering safer communities, protecting national security, and ensuring the health and well-being of all individuals, contributing to a more resilient and cohesive society.

Section 17.2: Policy Responses and Enforcement Mechanisms

17.2.1: Review of Existing Immigration Laws and Policies

The landscape of U.S. immigration law and policy is complex, shaped by decades of legislative changes, executive actions, and judicial decisions. Central to the discussion of unauthorized immigration is the Illegal Immigration Reform and Immigrant Responsibility Act (IIRIRA) of 1996, a pivotal piece of legislation that has had a profound impact on unauthorized immigrants and the enforcement of border security.

Impact of IIRIRA: The IIRIRA significantly transformed the U.S. immigration system, introducing stringent measures aimed at curbing unauthorized immigration. Key provisions included the expedited removal of certain unauthorized immigrants, increased penalties for immigration-related offenses, and the introduction of the 3-year, 10-year, and permanent bars on re-entry for individuals who had been unlawfully present in the U.S. Additionally, the act facilitated the expansion of physical barriers along the U.S.-Mexico border.

These measures have had far-reaching consequences for unauthorized immigrants, often resulting in the separation of families and making the path to legal status exceedingly difficult for those who had previously entered the U.S. without authorization. The act's punitive approach has also led to increased detentions and deportations, raising concerns about due process and human rights.

Challenges in Implementation: The implementation of IIRIRA has faced numerous challenges, including legal disputes over its interpretation, the logistical difficulties of enforcing expansive border security measures, and the humanitarian implications of its strict policies. Moreover, the act's focus on punitive measures has been criticized for failing to address the root causes of unauthorized immigration, such as the lack of legal pathways for immigration and the economic and safety factors driving individuals to migrate.

Calls for Reform: In response to these challenges, there have been persistent calls for comprehensive immigration reform. Critics of the current system argue for a more balanced approach that addresses border security and enforcement while also creating legal pathways for immigration, protecting the rights of asylum seekers, and offering a pathway to legal status for unauthorized immigrants who have long-term ties to the U.S.

Reform advocates emphasize the need to modernize the U.S. immigration system to reflect current economic needs, humanitarian obligations, and the reality of mixed-status families. Proposals often include measures to address the backlog of visa applications, protect Dreamers (individuals brought to the U.S. as children), and ensure fair and humane treatment of asylum seekers and refugees.

Conclusion: The review of existing immigration laws, particularly the IIRIRA, highlights the complexity of managing unauthorized immigration while balancing security concerns, humanitarian obligations, and the practical realities of a globalized world. Effective immigration policy requires a nuanced understanding of the factors driving unauthorized immigration, as well as the economic, social, and cultural contributions of immigrants to U.S. society. As such, ongoing debates and efforts toward immigration reform reflect the search for a policy framework that is both effective and reflective of America's values as a nation of immigrants.

17.2.2: Detailed Description of Border Security Measures

The United States has employed a variety of border security measures over the years to prevent unauthorized immigration, drug trafficking, and other security threats. These measures have evolved from simple physical barriers to sophisticated surveillance technologies and deployment strategies.

Evolution of Border Security Measures:

- **Physical Barriers**: The construction of physical barriers along the U.S.-Mexico border has been a central element of border security strategy for decades. Initially consisting of simple fences and vehicle barriers, these have evolved into more substantial walls and fencing systems in key areas. The Secure Fence Act of 2006 marked a significant escalation in barrier construction, mandating the erection of hundreds of miles of additional fencing.

- **Surveillance Technologies**: In recent years, there has been a shift towards the use of advanced surveillance technologies. Drones, high-definition cameras, ground sensors, and radar systems are now deployed extensively to monitor border areas. These technologies allow for the detection of movements in remote and rugged terrains where physical barriers are not feasible.

- **Border Patrol Agents**: The number of Border Patrol agents has increased significantly since the early 1990s, reflecting a growing emphasis on manpower in border security efforts. These agents are responsible for patrolling the border, apprehending individuals attempting unauthorized entry, and conducting search and rescue operations.

Humanitarian and Ecological Impacts:

- **Humanitarian Concerns**: One of the most controversial aspects of border security measures, particularly the construction of physical barriers, is their impact on human rights and safety. Barriers and enhanced surveillance have been criticized for pushing migrants towards more dangerous routes through harsh environments, leading to increased fatalities and injuries. Additionally, the presence of barriers disrupts the lives of communities living along the border, affecting their daily activities and access to resources.

- **Ecological Impact**: The environmental impact of border security measures is another significant concern. Physical barriers and infrastructure development disrupt wildlife habitats, migration patterns, and water flows in border regions. Conservationists argue that the damage to ecosystems and biodiversity can be profound and irreversible, affecting both the United States and neighboring countries.

Assessment: While border security measures are deemed necessary for national security and the management of unauthorized immigration, their effectiveness and ethical implications are subjects of ongoing debate. Critics argue that a heavy reliance on physical barriers and enforcement activities does not address the root causes of migration and may exacerbate humanitarian crises at the border. Moreover, the environmental degradation resulting from these measures calls for a reevaluation of border security strategies, emphasizing the need for solutions that balance security objectives with humanitarian and ecological considerations.

In summary, as border security technologies and strategies continue to evolve, it is crucial to assess their impacts comprehensively, taking into account not only their effectiveness in deterring unauthorized entry but also their broader implications for human rights and the environment.

17.2.3: Discussion on the Interior Enforcement Strategies

Interior enforcement of immigration laws in the United States involves a range of activities aimed at identifying, detaining, and deporting unauthorized immigrants who are already in the country. This facet of immigration policy has been marked by controversy and debate, especially regarding its impact on communities and the role of local law enforcement.

Key Strategies for Interior Enforcement:

- **Workplace Raids**: Historically, workplace raids have been used as a tool for identifying and detaining unauthorized workers. These operations have sparked significant debate due to their disruptive impact on businesses and the immigrant community. Critics argue that such raids create a climate of fear, tearing families apart and destabilizing communities.

- **Deportation Policies**: Deportation policies have varied significantly across different administrations, with some focusing on deporting immigrants with criminal convictions while others have taken a broader approach. The implementation of these policies has profound implications for families and communities, often resulting in the separation of families with deep roots in the U.S.

- **Local Law Enforcement for Immigration Enforcement**: Programs that involve local law enforcement in immigration enforcement, such as the 287(g) program, have been particularly contentious. Supporters argue that these partnerships are essential for upholding immigration laws, while critics contend that they lead to racial profiling, undermine trust in law enforcement, and deter immigrants from reporting crimes or accessing essential services.

Effects on Communities and the Debate Over Sanctuary Cities:

- **Community Impact**: Interior enforcement strategies have had significant effects on immigrant communities, contributing to a climate of fear and uncertainty. Families often face the prospect of separation, and individuals may be reluctant to engage with law enforcement or seek essential services due to fears of detention and deportation. This atmosphere can strain community relations and impact public safety.

- **Sanctuary Cities**: In response to aggressive interior enforcement, some cities and states have adopted "sanctuary" policies, limiting cooperation with federal immigration authorities. Advocates of sanctuary cities argue that these policies are vital for protecting the rights of immigrants, maintaining public safety by fostering trust between law enforcement and communities, and focusing limited resources on serious crimes. Opponents, however, claim that sanctuary policies hinder the enforcement of federal immigration laws and potentially harbor criminals.

Evaluation:

The effectiveness and ethical implications of interior enforcement strategies remain subjects of intense debate. While proponents argue that these measures are necessary to enforce immigration laws and protect public safety, critics highlight the adverse effects on communities, including the disruption of families, the spread of fear, and the erosion of trust in law enforcement.

The debate over sanctuary cities encapsulates the broader national conversation about how to balance immigration enforcement with respect for individual rights and community relations. As the U.S. continues to grapple with these issues, finding a path forward requires carefully weighing the goals of enforcement against the values of compassion, family unity, and community trust.

Section 17.3: Addressing the Criminal and Public Health Concerns

17.3.1: Analysis of the Scope and Scale of Criminal Activities

Unauthorized immigration is often entangled with various criminal activities, complicating the enforcement landscape and raising significant humanitarian concerns. Among these, human smuggling and trafficking networks are particularly nefarious, exploiting vulnerable individuals seeking safe havens or better opportunities. Understanding and dismantling these networks require nuanced strategies that balance enforcement with protection for the victims.

Human Smuggling Networks:

- **Operations**: These networks are sophisticated, with operations spanning multiple countries. They exploit porous borders and use forged or stolen documents to facilitate the movement of people. The cost to migrants can be exorbitant, putting them in debt bondage or making them vulnerable to exploitation and abuse.
- **Risks to Migrants**: Migrants relying on smugglers often face dangerous journeys, risking death, injury, or abuse. The journey across hostile terrains, such as deserts or seas, without adequate resources, is perilous. Moreover, smugglers may abandon their charges in dangerous circumstances or hand them over to human traffickers.

Efforts to Combat Smuggling and Trafficking:

- **Law Enforcement Collaboration**: Combating human smuggling and trafficking networks requires international cooperation and collaboration between law enforcement agencies. This includes sharing intelligence, joint investigations, and operations to dismantle networks and prosecute those responsible.

- **Protection of Victims**: Efforts to address these criminal activities also involve identifying and protecting victims. This includes providing legal, psychological, and medical assistance to those rescued from smugglers and traffickers. Special visas and protection measures are often necessary to ensure the safety of victims who cooperate with law enforcement.
- **Public Awareness and Education**: Raising awareness about the dangers of engaging with smuggling networks and the legal avenues for migration can help reduce the reliance on these dangerous routes. Educational campaigns targeted at potential migrants and communities can inform about the risks and alternatives to using smugglers.

Challenges:

- **Distinguishing Between Smugglers and Victims**: A significant challenge in combating these networks is differentiating between the perpetrators and the victims. Migrants, often in desperate circumstances, may unknowingly become part of these networks, complicating legal proceedings and protection efforts.
- **Jurisdictional and Legal Hurdles**: The transnational nature of smuggling and trafficking rings presents jurisdictional challenges, requiring extradition agreements and harmonization of legal frameworks to effectively prosecute offenders and dismantle networks.

Cartels and Gang Involvement in Unauthorized Immigration:

- **Cartel Operations**: Cartels have diversified their operations to include human smuggling, leveraging their existing networks for drug trafficking. They control key routes into the United States and often force migrants to carry drugs, increasing the risks and consequences for the migrants involved.
- **Gang Recruitment**: Gangs, both in migrants' home countries and in the U.S., exploit vulnerable migrants for recruitment. This is particularly concerning for unaccompanied minors who may be targeted for their susceptibility and lack of familial protection.

Impact of Released Criminals Among Unauthorized Migrants:

- **Challenges in Monitoring**: Individuals with criminal backgrounds who re-enter the U.S. illegally pose significant challenges to public safety. The difficulties in tracking these individuals after their release from prison complicate efforts to mitigate potential threats.
- **Community Safety Measures**: Ensuring community safety involves a cooperative effort between immigration and local law enforcement to identify, monitor, and, when necessary, detain individuals who pose a risk to public safety.

Economic Vulnerabilities of Unauthorized Migrants:

- **Work Authorization Issues**: Unauthorized migrants who are unable to obtain legal work authorization face significant economic hardships. This lack of legal employment opportunities can lead to exploitation in the informal labor market and may push some towards illicit activities for survival.

- **Impact of Exhausted Assistance**: When temporary assistance or the goodwill of communities wears thin, those unable to legally work face acute vulnerabilities, including homelessness, which can have cascading effects on public health and safety.

The Potential for Increased Crime:

- **Economic Desperation**: The intersection of legal ineligibility for work and the cessation of any financial support creates conditions of desperation that can increase the likelihood of some individuals turning to crime, whether out of necessity or coercion.
- **Community and Law Enforcement Strategies**: Addressing these challenges requires proactive community support mechanisms and targeted law enforcement strategies that focus on prevention, integration support, and pathways to legal status where possible, to reduce the incentive for criminal activity.

Conclusion: The criminal activities associated with unauthorized immigration, including those perpetrated by cartels and gangs, pose significant challenges to public safety and national security. The economic desperation faced by unauthorized migrants without work authorization further compounds these challenges. Addressing these issues requires a comprehensive approach that includes international cooperation, robust law enforcement strategies, and policies aimed at reducing the vulnerabilities of unauthorized migrants. This approach must balance the need for security with the rights and dignity of individuals, aiming to integrate rather than marginalize vulnerable populations.

17.3.2: Review of Public Health Challenges

Barriers to Healthcare Access for Unauthorized Immigrants:

- Unauthorized immigrants often encounter significant barriers to accessing healthcare services. These include legal restrictions, language barriers, fear of deportation, and lack of knowledge about available services.
- The absence of health insurance due to ineligibility for most government-sponsored health plans exacerbates these issues, making even basic healthcare services financially prohibitive.

Implications for Public Health Systems:

- The limited access to preventive care and primary healthcare services for unauthorized immigrants can lead to more severe health issues becoming prevalent within this population. These conditions often require emergency medical attention, leading to higher costs for public health systems and emergency departments.
- Public health challenges, such as the spread of infectious diseases, are exacerbated when large segments of the population are outside the healthcare system. This not only affects the health of unauthorized immigrants but also poses risks to the broader community.

Solutions for Integrating Health Services:

- **Community Health Initiatives**: Local health departments and community organizations can play a crucial role in providing health education and services to unauthorized immigrants. Mobile health clinics and health fairs are effective strategies for reaching out to communities that are otherwise underserved.
- **Language and Cultural Competency**: Developing language and culturally competent health services can help to overcome barriers to healthcare access. Training for

healthcare providers in cultural competency and the provision of translation services are essential components of this approach.

Ensuring Equitable Access:

- **Policy Reforms**: Advocating for policy reforms that expand access to healthcare for all residents, regardless of immigration status, is critical for addressing public health challenges. State-level initiatives can provide models for expanding coverage and access.
- **Integrated Health Services**: Creating integrated health services that are specifically designed to address the needs of unauthorized immigrants can help to ensure more comprehensive and effective care. This includes mental health services, which are often overlooked but critically needed.
- **Public-Private Partnerships**: Collaborations between government agencies, non-profit organizations, and private sector partners can provide resources and innovative solutions for expanding healthcare access to marginalized populations.

Conclusion: The public health challenges associated with unauthorized immigration are significant but not insurmountable. Addressing these challenges requires a multifaceted approach that includes community engagement, policy reform, and the development of healthcare services that are accessible and responsive to the needs of unauthorized immigrants. By ensuring equitable access to health services, public health systems can better serve the entire community, leading to improved health outcomes and reduced healthcare costs.

17.3.3: Strategies for Enhancing Interagency Cooperation

Introduction: Enhancing interagency cooperation is essential for addressing the multifaceted challenges associated with unauthorized immigration, especially regarding public safety, national security, and public health. Effective collaboration between immigration enforcement agencies, local public health authorities, law enforcement, and community organizations can lead to more comprehensive and humane approaches to these issues.

Key Strategies for Enhancing Interagency Cooperation:

1. **Establishing Formal Partnerships and Communication Channels:**

   - Develop formal agreements and partnerships that define the roles and responsibilities of each participating agency or organization. This clarity can prevent overlap and ensure that resources are utilized efficiently.
   - Establish dedicated communication channels to facilitate the timely exchange of information and coordination of responses to emerging situations.

2. **Joint Training Programs:**

   - Implement joint training programs for personnel from different agencies to foster mutual understanding of each agency's operational procedures, legal frameworks, and challenges. Such training can improve coordination during joint operations and initiatives.
   - Include cultural competency and sensitivity training to ensure all personnel are equipped to engage effectively with diverse communities, including unauthorized immigrants.

3. **Community Engagement Initiatives:**

- Collaborate on community engagement initiatives that aim to build trust between unauthorized immigrants and law enforcement, healthcare providers, and public officials. Trust is critical for effective public health interventions and for ensuring community safety.
- Use community liaison officers and health advocates who can navigate both the needs of the unauthorized immigrant communities and the objectives of public agencies.

4. **Data Sharing Agreements:**

- Develop secure and privacy-compliant data-sharing agreements that allow agencies to share relevant information. This can improve the identification of public health trends, potential safety threats, and opportunities for intervention without compromising individual rights.
- Ensure that data-sharing practices adhere to legal and ethical standards to protect individuals' privacy and rights.

5. **Integrated Response Plans:**

- Create integrated response plans for public health emergencies, criminal activities, and other situations that require a coordinated approach. These plans should outline how different agencies will work together, share resources, and respond to incidents involving unauthorized immigrants.
- Regularly update and rehearse these plans to ensure readiness and effectiveness.

6. **Funding and Resource Allocation for Joint Initiatives:**

- Secure funding and allocate resources specifically for joint initiatives that address issues related to unauthorized immigration. This could include grants for community health programs, public safety projects, and educational outreach.
- Explore opportunities for federal, state, and private funding to support these collaborative efforts.

Conclusion: Enhancing interagency cooperation is pivotal in creating a more effective, humane, and holistic approach to managing the challenges associated with unauthorized immigration. By implementing these strategies, agencies can better address public health concerns, enhance public safety, and promote a more inclusive and supportive environment for all community members, including unauthorized immigrants.

Section 17.4: International Cooperation and Diplomatic Solutions

17.4.1: The Role of International Cooperation

Introduction: Addressing the root causes of unauthorized immigration requires a commitment to international cooperation and collaborative solutions. By engaging in partnerships and initiatives that target the underlying factors driving migration, such as economic instability, violence, and political unrest, countries can reduce the pressures that compel individuals to migrate. This section explores successful examples of international cooperation focused on economic development, anti-corruption efforts, and support for stabilizing governments.

Economic Development Programs:

- **Case Study: The European Union Trust Fund for Africa (EUTF):** Established to address the root causes of irregular migration and displaced persons in Africa, the EUTF supports projects that aim to create jobs, improve management of migration flows, and foster stability and security. Programs under the EUTF have contributed to job creation, vocational training, and the development of small and medium-sized enterprises (SMEs), showing how investment in economic development can directly impact migration patterns.

- **Central American Regional Security Initiative (CARSI):** The United States has funded CARSI to combat drug trafficking, gang violence, and economic instability in Central America. By improving security and rule of law, these efforts aim to create a safer and more prosperous region, reducing the compulsion for individuals to migrate.

Anti-Corruption Efforts:

- **United Nations Convention Against Corruption (UNCAC):** As the only legally binding international anti-corruption instrument, UNCAC promotes measures to prevent corruption, including transparency in government procurement and the protection of whistleblowers. By addressing corruption, countries can improve governance and economic development, which in turn can reduce the push factors for migration.

- **Transparency International:** Through its global network, Transparency International works with governments and civil society to design and implement anti-corruption programs. These efforts help to ensure that resources meant for economic development reach their intended recipients, thus improving living conditions and reducing the need for migration.

Support for Stabilizing Governments:

- **The Marshall Plan for Middle East Stability:** Drawing inspiration from the post-World War II Marshall Plan, proposals for a new Marshall Plan aim to rebuild and stabilize conflict-affected regions in the Middle East. By providing financial assistance, technical support, and capacity building, the initiative seeks to restore infrastructure, governance, and economic systems, addressing some of the root causes of displacement and migration.

- **Peacebuilding Support in Colombia:** International support for peace processes in Colombia, including efforts by the United Nations and various countries, has focused on ending decades of conflict and building a stable, peaceful society. By addressing the violence that has displaced millions within the country and driven migration, these efforts highlight the importance of international cooperation in creating conditions that allow people to thrive in their home countries.

Conclusion: International cooperation plays a critical role in addressing the root causes of unauthorized immigration by fostering economic development, combating corruption, and supporting the stabilization of governments. Through targeted initiatives and partnerships, the global community can create sustainable solutions that not only mitigate the need for migration but also contribute to a more secure and prosperous world for all.

17.4.2: Diplomatic Efforts to Address Root Causes

Introduction: Diplomatic efforts play a pivotal role in addressing the root causes of migration. By employing a combination of foreign aid, trade agreements, and support for conflict resolution, countries like the United States can mitigate the pressures that drive migration. This section examines the diplomatic strategies that have been or could be employed to create more stable and prosperous conditions in migrant-origin countries.

Foreign Aid and Development Assistance:

- **Targeted Foreign Aid:** The United States has a long history of using foreign aid to promote economic development and stability in countries from which significant migration flows originate. Aid is often directed towards improving education, healthcare, and economic infrastructure, aiming to tackle the direct causes of migration. For instance, the U.S. Agency for International Development (USAID) programs in Central America focus on enhancing economic opportunities, reducing violence, and strengthening governance.

- **Conditional Aid:** Implementing foreign aid with specific conditions related to governance reforms and anti-corruption measures encourages countries to undertake necessary internal changes. This approach ensures that aid effectively contributes to creating a conducive environment for economic growth and stability, thereby reducing migration pressures.

Trade Agreements:

- **Promoting Economic Stability Through Trade:** Trade agreements can be a powerful tool for promoting economic stability and growth in migrant-origin countries. By granting preferential access to markets, such agreements can spur economic development and create jobs. The United States-

Mexico-Canada Agreement (USMCA) includes provisions designed to improve labor conditions and environmental standards, illustrating how trade agreements can address some of the socio-economic issues that contribute to migration.

- **Building Economic Partnerships:** Beyond traditional trade agreements, building comprehensive economic partnerships that include provisions for workforce development and investment can further help in stabilizing economies. Such partnerships not only foster economic growth but also build stronger socio-political ties that can support collaborative migration management efforts.

Support for Conflict Resolution:

- **Diplomatic Engagement in Peace Processes:** The U.S. has played significant roles in diplomatic efforts aimed at resolving conflicts that drive migration. Supporting peace negotiations, facilitating dialogue between conflicting parties, and providing post-conflict reconstruction aid are crucial in creating conditions that allow displaced persons to return home or remain safely within their countries.

- **International Coalitions:** Forming or supporting international coalitions to address conflicts and crises that lead to large-scale migration is another effective diplomatic strategy. For example, the U.S. involvement in international coalitions against terrorism and support for NATO operations in conflict zones are efforts aimed at restoring peace and stability, thereby addressing one of the root causes of displacement and migration.

Conclusion: Diplomatic efforts to mitigate the root causes of migration involve a multifaceted approach that includes targeted foreign aid, strategic trade agreements, and active support for conflict resolution. By fostering economic development, encouraging good governance, and contributing to global peace and stability, such diplomatic strategies can significantly reduce the pressures that compel individuals to undertake risky migrations. Engaging in these efforts requires long-term commitment and collaboration with international partners, emphasizing diplomacy's essential role in creating a more just and stable world.

17.4.3: Case Studies of Successful Initiatives

Introduction: Effective bilateral and multilateral initiatives serve as compelling evidence of how targeted strategies can address the root causes of migration and foster stability and prosperity in migrant-origin regions. This section highlights key case studies that demonstrate successful outcomes from cooperation between the United States and other nations or regions.

Case Study 1: U.S.-Mexico Development Cooperation Framework

- **Overview:** The U.S.-Mexico Development Cooperation Framework is a bilateral initiative designed to address economic disparities and security concerns that contribute to migration. The framework focuses on economic development, education, and job creation in Mexico's southern regions and in Central America.
- **Key Outcomes:** The initiative has led to increased investment in infrastructure projects, vocational training programs, and small business development in Mexico's economically disadvantaged areas. These efforts aim to create sustainable employment opportunities and reduce the economic incentives for migration.
- **Lessons Learned:** The importance of addressing economic inequality as a root cause of migration is a critical takeaway. Investments in local economies can lead to significant improvements in living conditions, thereby reducing the push factors for migration. Collaboration and shared responsibility are key to the success of such initiatives.

Case Study 2: The Alliance for Prosperity Plan in the Northern Triangle

- **Overview:** The Alliance for Prosperity Plan is a joint initiative by the United States, Guatemala, Honduras, and El Salvador. Launched to stimulate economic growth, improve security, and strengthen governance in the Northern Triangle countries, the plan aims to tackle the drivers of migration at their source.
- **Key Outcomes:** Notable achievements include strengthening public institutions, enhancing regional security cooperation, and implementing significant infrastructure projects that have created jobs and improved access to essential services.
- **Lessons Learned:** Effective governance and regional security collaboration are crucial for creating an environment conducive to economic development and stability. International support, when aligned with local needs and priorities, can facilitate meaningful progress towards reducing migration pressures.

Case Study 3: Regional Migration Management Agreements

- **Overview:** Agreements like the Bali Process on People Smuggling, Trafficking in Persons, and Related Transnational Crime exemplify regional cooperation in managing migration and addressing its underlying causes. These agreements focus on enhancing border security, combatting human trafficking, and ensuring safe, orderly, and regular migration.
- **Key Outcomes:** Enhanced information sharing and cooperation on law enforcement have led to significant crackdowns on human trafficking networks. Capacity-building efforts have improved national and regional frameworks for managing migration more humanely and effectively.

- **Lessons Learned:** The complexity of migration issues requires a comprehensive approach that includes both security measures and mechanisms to ensure the protection of migrants' rights. Regional cooperation is essential for addressing transnational challenges and ensuring that migration is safe, orderly, and beneficial for all involved.

Conclusion: These case studies illustrate the potential for bilateral and multilateral initiatives to make meaningful progress in addressing the root causes of migration. By focusing on economic development, security, governance, and regional cooperation, these initiatives offer valuable lessons for future efforts to manage migration in a way that benefits migrant-origin and destination countries alike. Success hinges on the commitment to shared goals, flexibility in addressing evolving challenges, and the integration of lessons learned into ongoing and new initiatives.

Section 17.5: Recommendations for Policy Reform and Future Directions

17.5.1: Proposals for Reforming the Immigration System

Introduction: The U.S. immigration system, characterized by its complexities and inefficiencies, calls for comprehensive reform. Addressing the current challenges requires a multifaceted approach that not only ensures the integrity and security of the nation but also upholds the dignity and rights of migrants. This section outlines key proposals for overhauling the immigration system.

Creating Legal Pathways for Migration:

- **Expand Visa Categories:** Increase the number and types of visas available to address the diverse needs of migrants, including work, family reunification, and humanitarian protections. This expansion should be responsive to labor market demands and demographic trends.
- **Streamline Application Processes:** Simplify visa application processes to make them more accessible and efficient. Reducing processing times and costs can alleviate backlogs and discourage unauthorized migration.
- **Temporary Protected Status (TPS) Reforms:** Enhance the TPS program to provide clearer pathways to permanent residency for beneficiaries, recognizing the often-prolonged nature of conditions that prevent safe return to home countries.

Reforming the Asylum Process:

- **Increase Asylum Officer Capacities:** Boost the number of trained asylum officers to expedite the initial screening of asylum claims, reducing the backlog in immigration courts.

- **Community-Based Alternatives to Detention:** Implement alternatives to detention for asylum seekers, focusing on community support and case management, to ensure humane treatment while maintaining compliance with legal proceedings.
- **Enhance Legal Representation:** Guarantee access to legal representation for asylum seekers, particularly for vulnerable populations such as children and victims of trauma or persecution, to ensure fair proceedings.

Ensuring the Humane Treatment of Migrants:

- **End Family Separation:** Permanently end the practice of family separation at the border and ensure that detention policies prioritize the welfare and rights of children and families.
- **Detention Standards and Oversight:** Implement and enforce higher standards for the treatment of migrants in detention, including healthcare access, and establish independent oversight mechanisms to ensure accountability.
- **Health and Safety Protocols:** Develop comprehensive health and safety protocols for processing and holding migrants, especially in light of public health concerns, to protect both migrants and border personnel.

Deportation of Criminals and Individuals with Severe Health Issues:

- **Prioritize the Removal of Criminals:** Reform policies to prioritize the deportation of individuals convicted of serious crimes, ensuring that the immigration system effectively protects public safety. This approach should focus on individuals who pose a genuine and significant threat to security, rather than broad categories that can lead to the unjust removal of individuals with minor offenses.

- **Assess and Address Severe Health Cases:** Establish clear guidelines for the assessment and handling of cases involving severe health issues, ensuring that decisions are made based on comprehensive medical evaluations and human rights considerations. Deportation should be considered when an individual's health condition poses a public health risk that cannot be effectively managed within the U.S., and if appropriate care and support can be assured in the individual's country of origin.

- **Expedite Cases of Individuals Wanted in Their Nation of Origin:** Implement procedures to expedite the review and potential deportation of individuals wanted for serious crimes in their country of origin, in accordance with international law and human rights standards. This process must include robust legal protections to ensure that individuals are not returned to situations where they would face persecution, torture, or other violations of their rights.

Implementing Safeguards and Due Process:

- **Enhance Due Process Protections:** Strengthen due process protections for individuals facing deportation, ensuring that they have access to legal representation and a fair opportunity to contest their removal, especially in cases involving criminal allegations or complex health considerations.

- **International Cooperation and Human Rights Compliance:** Enhance cooperation with international agencies and the countries of origin to ensure that deportations are carried out in compliance with international human rights obligations. This includes verifying that returnees will not face persecution or inhumane treatment and that health cases are managed with dignity and care.

- **Transparency and Accountability:** Increase transparency and accountability in the deportation process, including clear reporting on the criteria used for prioritizing deportations, the outcomes of deportation proceedings, and the measures in place to protect the rights and welfare of deportees.

Conclusion:

Incorporating these additional measures into the broader proposals for reforming the U.S. immigration system emphasizes the need to balance enforcement with compassion and respect for human rights. Prioritizing the deportation of individuals who pose a genuine threat, while ensuring due process and safeguarding against human rights violations, is crucial for maintaining the integrity and fairness of the immigration system.

17.5.2: Recommendations for a Balanced Approach to Enforcement

Balancing Security, Efficiency, and Human Rights:

- **Targeted Enforcement Priorities with Exceptions:** While prioritizing the deportation of individuals with serious criminal records, it's crucial to establish clear exceptions. These exceptions should apply to individuals who do not qualify for protections due to their criminal history, severe health concerns, or being wanted for serious crimes in their nation of origin. This targeted approach ensures resources are not wasted on those who pose a risk to public safety, thereby allowing for a more efficient use of resources in managing migration.

- **Charging Origin Countries for Releasing Criminals:** Implement policies to hold countries accountable that knowingly release criminals into the U.S. immigration system. This could involve diplomatic measures, economic sanctions, or charging fees to these nations to cover the costs of detention, processing, and deportation. Such measures would encourage better cooperation and responsibility-sharing in the management of global migration flows.

Improving Conditions and Oversight with Strategic Exceptions:

- **Selective Application of Detention Standards:** While advocating for improvements in detention conditions, it's essential to recognize that individuals with a history of violent crime or those posing a security threat may require stricter detention measures. However, these measures should still adhere to basic human rights standards, emphasizing the need for safety and security within these facilities.

- **Independent Oversight with Focus on High-Risk Facilities:** Prioritize independent oversight for facilities detaining high-risk individuals, ensuring these centers adhere to strict standards due to the potential danger posed by their detainees. This targeted oversight approach allows for a more efficient allocation of monitoring resources while upholding human rights standards.

Refining Legal and Supportive Measures:

- **Prioritized Legal Representation:** Focus on providing legal representation to detainees who do not fall under the specified exceptions, ensuring those with valid claims to stay in the U.S. have access to justice. This prioritization helps allocate legal aid resources more effectively, ensuring that individuals with a potential positive impact on society receive the support they need.

- **Trauma-Informed Care with Caveats:** Implement trauma-informed care, with an understanding that certain individuals, due to their criminal actions, may not fully benefit from such approaches. Tailor these practices to support the majority of migrants who have fled violence and persecution, while considering the security measures necessary for those posing a threat.

Conclusion

A balanced approach to enforcement in the U.S. immigration system involves prioritizing public safety and national security, upholding human rights, and ensuring the efficient use of resources. By focusing on targeted enforcement with clear exceptions, improving detention conditions with strategic oversight, and refining legal and supportive services, the U.S. can manage migration more effectively and humanely. Holding origin countries accountable for contributing to challenges within the U.S. immigration system encourages international cooperation and shared responsibility in addressing global migration issues.

Section 17.6: Conclusion

17.6.1: Summary of the Importance of a Multifaceted Approach

In addressing the complex challenge of unauthorized immigration, it has become increasingly clear that no single policy or approach can provide a sustainable solution. Throughout this exploration, the necessity for a comprehensive, multifaceted strategy has been underscored, one that equally weighs enforcement measures with humanitarian considerations and systemic reforms. This balanced approach is not only crucial for upholding the principles of justice and human dignity but also for enhancing the effectiveness and fairness of the immigration system as a whole.

Enforcement efforts, while necessary for maintaining national security and public safety, must be judiciously applied and accompanied by policies that respect the human rights of all individuals. Simultaneously, humanitarian aid and protections for vulnerable populations, including asylum seekers and refugees, must be integral components of our immigration policy, reflecting our values and international obligations.

Systemic reforms are equally critical. By addressing the root causes of unauthorized immigration, such as economic disparity, violence, and political instability in home countries, alongside improving legal pathways for immigration, the U.S. can reduce the pressures that compel individuals to migrate under perilous conditions. These reforms must also include modernizing the immigration system to make it more efficient, fair, and responsive to the changing dynamics of global migration.

The chapters have illuminated the interconnectivity of public safety, national security, public health, and the economic and societal contributions of immigrants. A policy framework that recognizes these interdependencies, and seeks to balance them, is essential for the creation of a more secure, prosperous, and equitable society.

In conclusion, the challenge of unauthorized immigration calls for a response that is as dynamic and multifaceted as the issue itself. By embracing a strategy that combines enforcement with compassion, and systemic reforms with international cooperation, the U.S. can better navigate the complexities of global migration in the 21st century, fostering a future that benefits both the nation and the global community at large.

17.6.2: A Call to Action

As we stand at a crossroads, facing the enduring and evolving challenges of unauthorized immigration, the path forward requires more than mere policy adjustments; it demands a collective commitment to reimagining our approach to immigration. This call to action is not just for policymakers but for all segments of society: civil society, the private sector, communities, and every individual. Together, we have the power and the responsibility to shape an immigration system that reflects the best of our values as a nation—justice, compassion, and respect for human dignity—while also fulfilling our international responsibilities.

To move forward, we must engage in open, constructive dialogue that transcends political divisions and focuses on finding sustainable, humane solutions to the complex issues of unauthorized immigration. This dialogue should be informed by evidence, guided by empathy, and aimed at achieving practical outcomes that balance security with humanity, and lawfulness with compassion.

Civil society organizations, with their on-the-ground experience and expertise, are invaluable in this conversation, offering insights into the human impact of policies and proposing innovative solutions. The private sector, too, plays a critical role in highlighting the economic implications of immigration policies and advocating for reforms that support economic growth and competitiveness.

Communities across the nation, especially those most directly affected by immigration, must also have a voice in this process, sharing their experiences, concerns, and aspirations. And at the individual level, every American can contribute to this dialogue by staying informed, challenging misconceptions, and advocating for policies that align with our values and interests.

Ultimately, the goal is to craft an immigration system that is fair, efficient, and humane; one that secures our borders, respects the rights of all individuals, and harnesses the contributions of immigrants to our society. Achieving this goal is not only in the best interest of the United States but also contributes to a more stable, prosperous, and just world.

This is a moment for bold action and visionary leadership. Let us come together to uphold America's legacy as a nation of immigrants and a beacon of hope, freedom, and opportunity for people from around the globe. The journey ahead is undoubtedly challenging, but with collective will and unwavering commitment to our shared values, we can forge a brighter, more inclusive future for America and beyond.

ACT PROPOSAL

TITLE I: National Immigration Reform Act

An Act to provide comprehensive reform regarding all persons who are unlawfully within the borders of the United States of America.

Section 1:

Establishment of a Joint Operational Task Force for Immigration Reform

Mandate the Department of Immigration and the Department of Justice to reallocate personnel, facilities, and all necessary equipment, along with jurisdictional mandates, to create a joint operational task force. This task force shall oversee the formation of an agency, or sub-agency, whose primary focus will be the implementation, oversight, and daily operations of the aforementioned agency/sub-agency (name to be determined later).

This entity will operate in conjunction with, yet independently from, the Department of Immigration and the Department of Justice. Its purpose is to facilitate an Inmate Work to Release Program, as permitted by the Thirteenth Amendment, Section 1: "Neither slavery nor involuntary servitude, except as punishment for crime whereof the party shall have been duly convicted..."

Legal Reference: The creation of a joint operational task force can draw authority from the Homeland Security Act of 2002 (Pub.L. 107–296, 116 Stat. 2135), which established the Department of Homeland Security and allows for the coordination and unification of national efforts to secure the United States. The task force's formation and objectives would align with 6 U.S.C. § 112(b)(2), empowering the Secretary to establish and coordinate efforts for national security.

Section 2:

Jurisdiction and Mandate of the New Entity

This entity shall possess jurisdiction over all foreign-born individuals currently in any State or Federal penal facility, in holding, or within the justice system, including those convicted but awaiting sentencing, sentenced but awaiting implementation, or falling within the confines of probation and/or parole. Furthermore, this entity's mandate shall include the remand of all aforementioned individuals to the aforesaid Work to Release Program.

Additionally, all past, current, and future foreign-born individuals who have entered the United States through illegal means, are currently present on American soil, or who are detained, arrested, or otherwise held for crimes associated with illegal entry into the United States, or by other means are subject to judicial criminal sentencing for crimes related to illegal immigration into the United States, and who fall into the jurisdiction of any associated agency (be it the judicial system, Department of Immigration, State or Federal penal system, Border Patrol, the Department of Homeland Security, or any other such agencies) shall also fall under this entity's mandate.

Legal Reference: The jurisdiction and mandate could be structured under the Immigration and Nationality Act (INA; 8 U.S.C. §1101 et seq.), which provides a comprehensive framework for immigration law in the United States. Specifically, sections dealing with the detention and removal of aliens (e.g., 8 U.S.C. § 1227 - Deportable aliens) could be amended to include provisions for the proposed Work to Release Program.

Section 3:

International Cooperation and Work to Release Program Negotiations

This entity, in cooperation with the U.S. Department of State and other relevant agencies, shall engage in negotiations with the governments of countries whose citizens are participants in the Work to Release Program. The aim is to establish agreements that outline the rights and responsibilities of the parent nation, the foreign nationals held in custody, and the terms of the Work to Release Program, ensuring mutual cooperation and respect for sovereignty.

Legal Reference: The principle of international cooperation could be supported by the Vienna Convention on Consular Relations of 1963, which facilitates communication and cooperation between nations regarding nationals detained abroad. Additionally, bilateral agreements must comply with principles established under international law, including the International Covenant on Civil and Political Rights (ICCPR), ensuring that any work program respects the rights and dignity of the individuals involved.

Section 4:

Work to Release Program Agreements

Agreements concerning the Work to Release Program should mirror the program's mandates closely. Participants in the Work to Release Program will be required to engage in labor as part of their rehabilitation and restitution process for a term not less than two years. Upon completion, individuals shall be repatriated to their country of citizenship, which will then assume responsibility for their reintegration, possibly through a similar program, as outlined in international agreements.

Legal Reference: The agreements for the Work to Release Program must adhere to standards set by the International Labour Organization (ILO) conventions, specifically the Forced Labour Convention (No. 29) and the Abolition of Forced Labour Convention (No. 105), to ensure that any labor is not coerced and respects the human rights of the participants.

Section 5:

Program Structure and Duration

The proposed structure of the agreement encompasses two years of labor and service within the Work to Release Program in the United States, followed by an additional two years within the jurisdiction of the participant's home country, as agreed upon. This bilateral approach aims at ensuring a comprehensive rehabilitation and restitution process.

Legal Reference: This component of the program would need to ensure compliance with the Fair Labor Standards Act (FLSA; 29 U.S.C. § 201) regarding the treatment and payment of workers, to the extent applicable. While the Thirteenth Amendment permits involuntary servitude as a punishment for crime, any labor conditions must still adhere to recognized standards for humane treatment.

Section 6:

Legal and Ethical Framework

The Work to Release Program will operate under the legal and ethical frameworks established by the Thirteenth Amendment and relevant legal precedents. It will focus on infrastructure improvement and community service projects beneficial to the public interest, with strict adherence to human rights standards.

Legal Reference: The ethical and legal framework for the Work to Release Program draws upon the Thirteenth Amendment to the United States Constitution. Additionally, the program must conform to the standards outlined in the Universal Declaration of Human Rights, particularly Articles 4 and 23, which address freedom from slavery and servitude and the right to work, respectively.

Section 7:

Post-Program Repatriation and Cooperation

Upon successful completion of the program within the United States, the participants will be transferred under the terms agreed upon with their home countries. The goal is to facilitate a seamless transition that supports the participants' reintegration into their societies, potentially through continued work and service aligned with their countries' needs and interests.

Legal Reference: Repatriation agreements should be guided by international law principles found in the Convention on the Rights of the Child (CRC, specifically Article 10 concerning family reunification) and the International Covenant on Civil and Political Rights (ICCPR, Article 12, regarding the right to enter one's country).

Section 8:

Governing Board and Program Oversight

A governing board, representing various stakeholders, will be established to oversee the Work to Release Program, ensuring compliance with legal standards, ethical considerations, and the achievement of program objectives. This board will also be responsible for the detailed planning and execution of the program, including its operational aspects.

Legal Reference: The governance and oversight mechanisms can be modeled after existing federal agency oversight provisions, such as those found in the Inspector General Act of 1978 (Pub.L. 95–452), which established Offices of Inspectors General within federal agencies to prevent fraud, waste, and abuse.

Section 9:

Program Features and Support Services

The Work to Release Program will include a comprehensive support system for participants, encompassing vocational training, housing, healthcare, and other necessary services to ensure their well-being and successful reintegration. Security and monitoring measures will be implemented to protect both the participants and the community.

Legal Reference: The support services component should align with the Rehabilitation Act of 1973 (29 U.S.C. § 701), emphasizing the need to support the rehabilitation and reintegration of individuals through vocational training, education, and other services.

Section 10:

Eligibility and Exclusions

Criteria for participation in the Work to Release Program will be clearly defined, with exclusions for individuals deemed a high risk to public safety, including those with a history of violent crime or classified as flight risks.

Legal Reference: Eligibility criteria must conform to constitutional protections against discrimination, as outlined in the Equal Protection Clause of the 14th Amendment. Criteria for exclusions, particularly regarding public safety, can draw on legal standards established in cases like Zadvydas v. Davis, 533 U.S. 678 (2001), which addressed the detention of aliens under immigration laws.

Section 11:

Financial Responsibility and Restitution Assessment

An integral component of the Work to Release Program involves a thorough assessment of each participant's financial impact on the U.S. stemming from their illegal activities. This will include, but not be limited to, unpaid taxes, the use of state and federal aid, and the costs associated with legal proceedings and detention. A comprehensive review will ascertain the total financial obligation of each individual, which will then be addressed through their participation in the program.

Legal Foundation: The concept of restitution is supported by various legal precedents, such as the Mandatory Victims Restitution Act of 1996 (18 U.S.C. § 3663A), which requires convicted offenders to pay restitution to their victims as part of their sentence. Although primarily applied within a domestic context, the principle can be extended to address financial impacts of illegal immigration.

Section 12:

Compensation and Financial Management

Participants will receive compensation for their labor at a rate determined by the program's guidelines, reflecting the nature of the work and ensuring fairness. Earnings will be managed through a designated account, with a portion allocated directly towards covering the costs of the program and the individual's financial obligations. Upon satisfying these obligations and completing the program, participants will have access to the remaining funds, providing a foundation for their future endeavors post-repatriation.

Legal Framework: The Fair Labor Standards Act (29 U.S.C. § 201) ensures that workers receive at least the federal minimum wage and overtime. While this act primarily applies to legal workers, its ethical foundation underpins the compensation structure proposed in the program, ensuring fairness and compliance with basic labor standards.

Section 13:

Ongoing Evaluation and Adaptation

To ensure the Work to Release Program achieves its intended goals, an ongoing evaluation mechanism will be established. This will allow for continuous assessment of program effectiveness, participant well-being, and community impact. Feedback loops will enable timely adjustments to program operations, ensuring responsiveness to the needs of participants and the broader societal objectives.

Accountability Mechanism: The Government Performance and Results Act of 1993 requires federal agencies to demonstrate accountability through strategic planning and performance reporting. This act supports the section's emphasis on ongoing evaluation and adaptation, ensuring that the program meets its objectives efficiently.

Section 14:

Transparency and Accountability

Maintaining transparency and accountability throughout the program's implementation is paramount. Regular reporting to relevant governmental bodies, stakeholders, and the public will be mandated, covering program metrics, successes, challenges, and financial audits. This will foster trust and ensure that the program operates within its legal and ethical boundaries.

Following the enactment of this Act, individuals convicted of crimes falling under the Work to Release Program's jurisdiction will be integrated into the program, adhering to the established mandate and operational guidelines. This provision ensures a consistent approach to handling such cases, aligning with the Act's broader goals of rehabilitation and societal reintegration.

Legal Precedent: The Freedom of Information Act (5 U.S.C. § 552) and the Privacy Act of 1974 (5 U.S.C. § 552a) establish the public's right to access government information while protecting individual privacy. These laws underscore the program's commitment to transparency and accountability to both the public and stakeholders.

Section 15:

Final Provisions

This act mandates the creation of a framework that not only addresses the immediate challenges of illegal immigration but also provides a structured and humane pathway for restitution and reintegration. Through international cooperation, robust legal and ethical oversight, and a commitment to the well-being of all participants, the Work to Release Program aims to serve as a model for comprehensive immigration reform.

By focusing on rehabilitation, restitution, and reintegration, this program seeks not only to address the consequences of illegal entry into the United States but also to contribute positively to the participants' futures and the countries involved. This act is a step toward a more equitable, just, and pragmatic approach to immigration reform.

In instances where restitution remains unpaid and the individual has successfully completed the Work to Release Program, the outstanding balance will be actively pursued for a period of seven years. If the individual re-offends with crimes under the jurisdiction of the Work to Release Program during this time, any previous unpaid restitution will be added to the new assessment, creating a consolidated financial obligation. Should the individual avoid further criminal convictions related to the program's scope for seven years post-release, the remaining restitution balance will be forgiven, underscoring the program's rehabilitative intent and its emphasis on encouraging lawful behavior.

Comprehensive Approach: While specific legal codes may not directly apply, this section embodies principles found in international human rights law, such as the right to work and the prohibition of forced labor (International Covenant on Economic, Social and Cultural Rights, Article 6 & 7; International Labor Organization Convention No. 29). These principles affirm the act's commitment to humane and ethical treatment.

Section 16

(Reform to a Pathway to Citizenship Program):

This section introduces a provision for foreign-born individuals currently residing in the U.S. illegally but not wanted for other crimes. It offers an amnesty period, starting the day after the Act's enactment, during which these individuals can voluntarily present themselves for processing. This period, determined by a Congressional Committee, aims to facilitate a structured pathway to legal residency, emphasizing the Act's balance between enforcement and compassion.

Legal Basis: The Immigration and Nationality Act (8 U.S.C. § 1101 et seq.) serves as the foundational legal framework for immigration policy in the United States. Modifications to provide a pathway to citizenship align with precedents such as the Deferred Action for Childhood Arrivals (DACA) program, which offers relief from deportation and work permits to eligible immigrants brought to the U.S. as children.

Section 17:

Qualifying individuals under Section 15 can choose to participate in the Pathway to Citizenship Program or face deportation. Eligibility requires agreement to specific terms, including self-sufficiency without reliance on most state or federal aid (excluding educational aid) for a total of 11 years, employment or full-time education, and maintaining a compliant residence. These criteria underscore the program's commitment to fostering responsible and contributing members of society.

Legal and Ethical Considerations: These sections draw on principles of rehabilitation and reintegration similar to those in the U.S. criminal justice system's probation and parole systems (18 U.S.C. § 3561 for probation; 18 U.S.C. § 4205 for parole), focusing on monitoring and gradual reintegration into society.

Section 18:

The Pathway to Citizenship Program consists of two phases: "Observation and Evaluation for Full Citizenship" and "Evaluated Immigrant to Citizen." This staged approach allows for a thorough assessment of participants' adherence to program stipulations and their integration into the community.

Section 18 (Part 1: Observation and Evaluation for Full Citizenship):

Participants agree to a morality clause, abstain from criminal activities, and undergo regular substance testing. They also commit to repaying any financial obligations related to their illegal stay, including taxes and received state or federal aid. This phase emphasizes personal responsibility and legal compliance as foundational elements of the pathway to citizenship.

Section 18 (Part 2: Evaluated Immigrant to Citizen):

This phase continues the evaluation process with eased restrictions on alcohol and reduced monitoring frequency, signifying progression towards full citizenship while maintaining the core commitments of the program.

Legal and Ethical Considerations: These sections draw on principles of rehabilitation and reintegration similar to those in the U.S. criminal justice system's probation and parole systems (18 U.S.C. § 3561 for probation; 18 U.S.C. § 4205 for parole), focusing on monitoring and gradual reintegration into society.

Section 19:

Legal infractions during the program can lead to enrollment in the Work to Release Program, highlighting the consequences of failing to adhere to the pathway's requirements and the importance of legal compliance for successful integration.

Section 20:

The Act becomes effective one business day after its provisions have been enacted and passed by Congress, setting a clear timeline for its implementation and operational commencement.

- **Implementation:** The Administrative Procedure Act (5 U.S.C. § 551 et seq.) guides the process of developing and enacting federal regulations, ensuring that new laws are implemented in a transparent, orderly, and efficient manner. This legal framework supports the act's clear timeline for implementation and operational commencement.

In drafting legislation such as the National Immigration Reform Act, it is critical to ensure that the proposed measures comply with existing legal frameworks and uphold constitutional and human rights standards. This analysis suggests that while ambitious, the act's provisions could be aligned with legal and ethical principles, provided they are implemented with careful consideration of fairness, transparency, and accountability.

ABOUT THE AUTHOR

FIN